jennifer moon

D0061270

Short Courses & Workshops

IMPROVING THE

IMPACT

OF LEARNING,

TRAINING &

PROFESSIONAL

DEVELOPMENT

**KOGAN
PAGE**

First published in 2001

Apart from any fair dealing for the purposes of research or private study, or criticism or review, as permitted under the Copyright, Designs and Patents Act 1988, this publication may only be reproduced, stored or transmitted, in any form or by any means, with the prior permission in writing of the publishers, or in the case of reprographic reproduction in accordance with the terms and licences issued by the CLA. Enquiries concerning reproduction outside these terms should be sent to the publishers at the undermentioned addresses:

Kogan Page Limited
120 Pentonville Road
London
N1 9JN
UK

Stylus Publishing Inc.
22883 Quicksilver Drive
Sterling
VA 20166-2012
USA

© Jennifer Moon, 2001

The right of Jennifer Moon to be identified as the author of this work has been asserted by her in accordance with the Copyright, Designs and Patents Act 1988.

British Library Cataloguing in Publication Data

A CIP record for this book is available from the British Library.

ISBN 0 7494 3266 7

Typeset by JS Typesetting, Wellingborough, Northants
Printed and bound in Great Britain by Clays Ltd, St Ives plc

Contents

Preface

This book has a number of features that distinguish it from much of the other literature in this field that might be termed post-16 education. There is a focus on a concern for the impact of short courses. The impact of a short course is the way in which the learning *on* the course is used *after* the course – often in a work situation. The general point is that unless a short course has an impact on practice, then there is probably little point in the learner embarking on the course.

The guarded use of the term 'post-16 education' belies another important feature of the book – it attempts to cut across at least three cultures in education – that of academic teaching, which is typically located in schools or in higher education, that of training, and that of adult education. Training tends to reside in the world of business or work organizations. While the training may seem to imply the learning of physical skills, many short training courses do not concern physical skills, but topics such as people management. Short courses found in the world of adult education are often community based, or emanate from programmes run for the community by educational institutions.

These three cultures of education, unfortunately use different sets of vocabulary. This causes problems in the choice of vocabulary for writing a book of this kind, which, one hopes, might have something to say to all three cultures, and this results in a compromise vocabulary. The existence of different cultures also has implications for the theoretical basis of short courses. There is a tendency for the literature to emanate from one culture or the other, and there is relatively little material that draws on all areas – as this book attempts to do. Looking at the literature, it can be difficult to believe that classroom education and that which occurs in the work training room have anything at all in common.

Another feature of this book that tends to distinguish it is its focus on the process of learning and not instruction (the compromise word used here for teaching/learning). The chapters on learning are used to form a basis for the discussion of instruction. In the latter half of the book, there is also reference to a new idea of a short course having components. A component is a group of potential activities on a course that can meet a common purpose. The introductory chapter outlines the content in a more detailed manner.

Another compromise is the choice of personal pronouns used. Being female, I am not keen to use masculine pronouns throughout all of the text. I am also not keen on the grammatical incorrectness that occurs if the gender is neutralized by making it plural through-out – or the confusion that tends to exist where a mix of masculine and feminine pronouns are used. I therefore compromise and use a feminine gender, except in reference to the material of others where gender has been implied.

There are thanks, of course, to be given. Many have been involved in facilitating the thinking that has lead to this book, and others have been involved in the book by default – I thank particularly Kyla and Shelley.

Introduction

Improving the impact of short courses and workshops

Introductory notes

This book is about the management of learning in short courses and workshops. We view short courses and workshops as forms of educational situations that are characterized both by their shortness and the fact that they have a place in a range of educational cultures. Of particular importance is that the aim of a short course is usually to achieve an impact – an improvement or change in some form of previous practice. 'Practice' is interpreted in a broad manner, though, for convenience, reference is often made to the workplace. This makes the text no less relevant to a craft learnt in an adult education class for practice at home.

This introduction is designed to set the scene for those that follow. The first section describes the influences that have shaped the writing of the book. The second section reviews the ideas that underpin its content and this leads into discussion of the fact that short courses and workshops are features of several educational settings. In order that the book be useful, the vocabulary that it employs has to be functional in different contexts and to achieve this some compromises have been made. The following section concerns the meanings of 'short courses' and 'workshops' in the context of this book. It reviews the conceptions of short course learning in the settings and cultures in which they occur. The last section of this introduction provides an overview of the content of the rest of the book.

The origins of the book

The book arose out of a number of experiences and observations gained over a period of years from involvement in short courses in academia, adult education, business, and professional and personal development. However, the main thinking was generated in relatively recent experience of developing short courses in health promotion in the National Health Service (NHS).

It was in the NHS that attention was drawn to the concept of the impact of a course on practice by the work of Kiely in 1988. Kiely had studied the Health Education Certificate Course, a year-long part-time course run by qualified professional health educationists for a range of professions such as nursing, teaching, dentistry, and the professions allied to medicine. These participants were seen as non-specialist in health promotion, but with opportunities in their practice to educate their clients for health. Kiely's work was concerned with the extent to which the learning from the course was eventually applied in the participant's practice – and she concluded that there was a problem with the impact of the course. People were participating, money was being spent on it and time was taken away from the workplace, but the learning, for a variety of reasons, was often not being put into practice (Kiely, 1988). The course was not having an impact.

At the time, I was working in a UK-wide project in which the aim was to improve the ability of non-specialists in health promotion to promote and educate for health in their own settings, HEA, HEBS, HPW, HPANI (Health Education Authority (England), Health Education Board for Scotland, Health Promotion Wales, Health Promotion Agency for Northern Ireland). The aim was to be achieved through short courses called 'Foundation' courses in health education/promotion. The client group was similar to that in Kiely's work, but this was a group that did not have the time or opportunity to engage in the Certificate Course. There was concern across the health promotion profession about what the content of these courses should be – and, more to the point, about their effectiveness. The courses usually ran from around 3 to about 20 days, but most were on the shorter side. In addition, there were many one-day courses that focused on specific topics. The interesting question was whether there were ways of increasing the impact of these courses on work practice. If there was not, then their existence should be questioned.

There was nothing unusual about this questioning in health promotion or in the National Health Service. There are many situations in which professional development occurs through short courses for which people are released from their workplace. It is not unusual for such courses to be evaluated on the basis of participants attending the course as opposed to an evaluation of the learning that results or – even more so – in improvement or change in workplace practice. In the case of the non-specialists in health promotion on these courses, there were frequent stories of how people had found difficulty in getting managers to agree to their attendance. When they returned from a course, they would find a backlog of work and unhelpful attitudes of colleagues who would imply that they had had a day 'off'. The day or two after a course is the time when people can still be excited by new ideas and ready to implement them. They need time and support from managers and colleagues to consider how to change their practice and hence they need a lower workload rather than a backlog to clear (HEA *et al*, 1995, Moon, 1996).

There were other events within my professional activities of that time that also raised consideration of how to work with people towards a particular 'end'. These were not short courses, but meetings or 'think-tanks' in which a group of people was working towards a decision or perhaps a discussion document. There were ineffective practices that seemed to parallel some of the processes within short courses. It became clear that bringing together a group of highly articulate professionals in a pleasant setting is not a guarantee of achieving a useful outcome. In these situations, for example, it was observed that:

> There is often conscientious planning of how information is to be gathered from participants (eg brainstorming, small group work etc), however, less time is given to the planning of the more difficult process of achieving consensus and making a clear conclusion. This may result in a series of half-considered statements. At the worst, workshop reports are derived from unprocessed flip chart jottings (and at the very worst someone who has not even attended the workshop writes up these jottings).
>
> (Moon and England, 1994)

Certainly, one of the factors that contributed to this situation was a myth, perhaps particularly rife among this group of professionals, that participants in meetings are not happy with a highly structured situation, which they would deem as dictatorial. The expected ethos was one of *laissez-faire*. In designing an effective decision-making situation, it was necessary to break through this myth and to expect that people would accept a structured situation if they felt that it would contribute to a good conclusion (Moon and England, 1994).

There was another influence for this book as well – the better use of reflection in courses. Over the years of involvement with professional development, ideas of the importance of reflection in learning and professional education were evolving. Reflection seemed to be significant in the process of learning on short courses, in linking learning on the course both to relevant prior practice in the workplace and to the anticipated change in the practice. The literature on reflection that might have been helpful was considerable in volume, but largely based in specific areas – in nurse education, teacher education in the literature on experiential learning, and in some more theoretical or philosophical contexts (eg, Habermas, 1971, Van Manen, 1977 and Barnett, 1997). I wrote a book as an attempt to pull together the literature on reflection into a more focused state, but also to relate it more properly to the literature on learning (Moon, 1999). This involved thinking about reflection in short courses. A further book followed on the use of learning journals – which touched on more practical areas of using reflection in learning, in professional development and in courses (Moon, 1999a).

Alongside the thinking that has been associated with writing and these areas of project activity, there has been the opportunity to put ideas into practice – at first in the context of further health promotion courses (Moon, 1996, 1998), and later in staff development in higher education. Subsequently there were opportunities to put together the ideas about improving impact in short courses in courses themselves on improving this impact.

Underpinning ideas

There are a number of ideas on which this book is based, most of which arise at several points in the text. The first, the notion of **impact**, is fundamental. The book is an analysis of the manner in which courses can more directly and positively affect the practice in which people engage after they have attended a short course. This might be in voluntary or paid work or in any topic that is addressed in adult education. For convenience, the model of 'impact' is based on the idea of a person returning to a work situation in order to do something new in her work – but its application is certainly wider. In the main, the effectiveness of a course in having impact on a workplace depends on the operation of many different features of a course. These are dealt with in the various sections of this book. In general, impact is influenced by:

- the manner in which aims and anticipated outcomes are expressed and used in the progress of a course (Chapter 1);
- the conception and understanding of the process of learning (Chapters 2, 3 and 4);
- the conception, understanding and operation of the process of instruction – and the manner in which this relates to the learning processes of learners (Chapters 5 and 6);
- the use of a framework for the design of the course that takes into account an understanding of the nature of relevant present practice, of the new learning, and which anticipates future changes in practice (Chapter 7);
- the way in which a variety of '**components**' of courses are managed (Chapter 8).

The notion of **course components** was developed in HEA, HEBS, HPW, HPANI (1995). Components are groups of activities that have a common role in courses. They can be seen as course activities, which are deployed at different times to achieve the identified purpose. There are, for example, various ways of summarizing the progress of a course, various ways of engendering group learning. While these activities form a 'toolkit' for the instructor, it is common for the attractiveness of the tools to dominate the concern for the purpose. While this may engender enjoyment, it does not necessarily have a great deal to do with the final impact of the learning on practice.

    The paragraph above is an example of another underpinning idea in this book – an attitude of **scepticism** about some of the literature on short courses. The literature is often lightweight and anecdotal, and not based on theory or principles. For example, many books on learning reach uncritically for the cycle of experiential learning (Kolb, 1984) – and do not go a lot further. There is also a tendency to capture training in systems diagrams where one box flows into another without consideration of how the flow occurs. An analysis of training need might flow into the development of a course, which flows into a 'course evaluation' box. It can be difficult to find the word 'learning' anywhere.

Adopting a stance of scepticism is no use without putting something in its place, so this book pays considerable attention to development of the **understanding of the process of learning** because the process of learning should be in the centre of short course development and operation. The book draws particularly on recent work on student learning because of its explanation and observation of learning behaviour. More significantly, this area of research provides useful guidance for practice in instruction. Key concepts in this approach to learning are '**deep**' and '**surface**' **approaches**. Deep learning is where the learner intends to learn in order to understand something; surface learning is where a learner simply tries to take in and memorize – without the intention to understand how ideas fit together or relate to prior knowledge or experience.

Good instruction, for example, will be guided substantially by the learning behaviour and performance of the learners (Trigwell and Prosser, 1999). The overt adoption of a learner-centred and **constructivist approach** in this account emphasizes the centrality of learning because it suggests that the learner constructs her new understandings and conceptions according to the manner in which she perceives the material to be.

The learner-centred view adopted has been derived from the work of such thinkers as Kelly (1955) and Rogers (1969). Kelly was the more extreme of the two. In his opinion, the learner constructs her view of the world on the basis of making sense of her own perceptions:

> …people understand themselves and their environment and anticipate future events, by constructing tentative models or personal theories of themselves and their environment, and by evaluating these theories against personal criteria as to whether the prediction and control of

events (based on the models) have been successful or not. All theories are hypotheses created by people. (Zuber-Skerritt, 1992, p 57).

Kelly considered humankind to act as scientist, perpetually developing ways of understanding events, testing those theories and rejecting, modifying or accepting them for the time being. He recognized that groups of people could share common views of the world (constructions of their experience) so they might have the same theories. He also believed that there is considerable variation in people's willingness to modify their theories in response to change – a factor of relevance to those in learning situations of their own or others' volition.

Ideas such as **precision**, **clarity** and **awareness** also underpin the development of this text. We have already said that there is much anecdotal writing about short courses. Because a short course is short, best use must be made of the time, both to help learners to learn and to ensure that they can then apply the learning in their workplaces. This puts pressure on the effective use of the resources such as the instructor and her processes of instruction and the facilitation of learning. While there is enormous native skill in facilitating learning, there are also deep understandings to be gained about how instruction and other aspects of the learning environment should align with the learners' processes of learning (Biggs, 1999). A short course needs to be underpinned by considerations that are both precise and clear about direction and the outcomes to be achieved, but are deployed within the context of continuous awareness of the state of learners and their learning.

There is no use in being aware of learners' processes unless there is the ability to respond to them. We introduced the idea of course components above. The idea of using 'components' of a course to achieve an identified purpose needs to be linked to a **holistic** view of the course. A course is not a haphazard collection of bits and pieces, but a carefully considered selection of tools that will enable the reaching of an identified point where the learning has impact on practice. Many of the components of a course are selected in advance and are used to facilitate particular areas of learning in appropriate manners. However, the ability to change in response to the learner's patterns also indicates the need for '**on the hoof flexibility**' – the ability to draw a useful but relevant activity in order to achieve the planned effect, while still moving forward towards the planned outcomes. An example is the use of alternative activities to those planned when the attention of learners is flagging. The activity should be relevant but perhaps different in pace, action or in demand from the learner.

A factor that reduces clarity and therefore precision in the fields of instruction and learning is the use of and, in some situations, the lack of **vocabulary**. Learners and instructors have different views of the process of learning and instruction. This emerges from constructivist theory and it directly impinges on attempts to align the processes of learning and instruction. Unless I, as an instructor, am aware of the view and expectations that you, as a learner, have of learning, how can I align my instruction to best facilitate your learning? Not only do instructors and learners construe instruction and learning words differently, but sometimes there is also missing vocabulary. One effect of this, for example, is to lead to confusion about the differences between the processes of instruction and learning (p 32). To overcome this difficulty some new vocabulary has been developed (see below).

Some compromises in vocabulary

A particular difficulty in writing this book that also has relevance to vocabulary is that short courses operate in many educational settings – in commercial or business training, in formal academic education and in the adult education sector. These sectors tend to operate with different views of learning and instruction (see above), are culturally different and use different vocabularies (see below). To write a book that usefully cuts across the cultural and vocabulary issues means that there will be compromises. Fortunately, at least we all talk of learning, but we use different words for the process of teaching/ training/tutoring. 'Teaching' as a word would not please trainers and likewise there is antipathy to the idea that educators in formal academic situations might engage in 'training'. We compromise and use the word 'instruction' and 'instructor'. These words are intended to relate to the process of facilitating learning in the best way. The terminology for course or workshop members is usually either 'learners' or participants.

Short courses, workshops and their settings

Short courses come in many shapes and forms and the definition of course or workshop addressed by this book is deliberately not specific. However, there are identifiable characteristics of short courses and workshops that make it worth writing a book such as this. Some of these characteristics are:

- Short courses and workshops are usually a few days in length at the most – because they are short there is a time constraint on the processes of learning and instruction.
- They are usually attended by a group of people who are together for a while. This can make group processes a relevant issue for both learning and teaching.
- Subject matter is usually concentrated (Parlett and King, 1971). In other words, learners do not study a variety of subjects but focus on one topic. This contrasts with most programmes of study.
- It is often the case that the instructor and learners do not know each other. The instructor is brought in to work with a group of learners who may or may not initially know each other.
- Most short courses involve a variety of activities. Some have come to appear regularly in short courses and to typify many courses – such as 'warm-ups', 'icebreakers' and so on.
- Cost-effectiveness may be a major factor.
- There may be an issue as to who is the customer of a short course. The customer might be regarded as an organization rather than the person who attends the course (Pithers, 1998).

The topic of this book – improving impact – suggests that courses are run for a purpose that has usually been considered before attendance.

Despite the general characteristics of short courses and workshops described above, much of what is contained in the following pages is relevant to longer courses, higher education modules or programmes. There is often little difference between a workshop and a short course, though workshops would usually have more participant activity, the nature of which will depend on the topic (Bourner, Martin and Race, 1993). For convenience, the main term used from here on is 'short courses', which will include the idea of workshops.

We have indicated that short courses and workshops occur in a number of settings – in particular in industrial and commercial training, in adult education and in formal academic situations. Rather than explaining and contrasting the different settings in text, we present the three compared on a number of points in a tabular format. This will provide a flavour of issues raised earlier that will be discussed at later stages of the book. Table 0.1 is compiled from many sources and it makes considerable generalization.

About the rest of the book

With reference to the notion of precision above, Chapter 1 introduces precision to the process of course development. In order to work towards a course having an impact, detailed and well-considered thinking is needed about what it is that the course is to achieve and how this relates to its structure. The chapter introduces the concepts of aims and learning outcomes and discusses the term 'objective'. It shows how aims might be derived from what we have called 'structuring factors', how aims and learning outcomes should relate to any assessment procedures and how this in turn relates to the process of instruction.

The quality of course participants' learning is central to the course development sequence discussed in Chapter 1 and to the achievement of impact. The next three chapters (Chapters 2, 3, and 4) consider aspects of learning that are particularly important for success in short courses. Chapter 2 reviews a number of factors that form the context for learning. These include the vocabulary of learning (initially including instruction because of the confusion that exists between the processes), common understandings and images of learning and their influence on learners, and the role of more formal views of learning. Another context of learning is the environment within which it occurs and the manner in which factors in the environment impinge on learning, particularly in short courses.

Chapter 3 looks in more detail at the quality of learning that is required to bring about impact on practice. It reviews the relatively recent work on approaches to learning and relates these to the results of learning in a 'map of learning and the representation of learning'.

Table 0.1 *Comparison of training, academic and adult education fields*

Training 'trainers'	Academic Education 'teachers'	Adult Education 'tutors'
experience may be assumed	experience generally not assumed	experience is assumed
attention paid to techniques of how learning might occur	tendency to assume that learners know how to learn – some work on study skills sometimes	general sense that learners know how to learn or will find the way that suits them
work more likely to be towards mastery	mastery not usually an aim – work towards modal performance or criteria of assessments set	what matters is that learner is satisfied with her learning (unless external assessment)
concern is usually for limited areas of learning – usually related to the current or future work	education – broad learning is expected as a basis for future development in work or as citizen	lead is taken from concerns of learner
experiential aspects of learning valued	experiential aspects of learning not necessarily valued	experiential aspects of learning valued
there is often a stated concern for individual differences in learners	generally not a stated concern for individual differences in learners	individual differences in learners is acknowledged
training of trainers tends to be specific and technique-based	education of teachers is more general	variable background of tutors
tendency to focus on one area of learning in a concentrated period of time	learning in many areas at the same time – learning not focused	one area of learning is usually dealt with at a time
cost-effectiveness of training and learning is overtly an issue	cost-effectiveness is not overtly taken into account	cost-effectiveness is not overtly an issue
sense of getting learners from state of not knowing about something to state of 'knowing'	concerns for personal development more general	concern is for person's needs for learning – whether narrow or broad

Differences between learners can be particularly significant in short courses because the mix of people can be considerable and because there may be little time for discrepancies in experience, ability or progress to be made up. Chapter 4 explores some of the differences that might be encountered and some means of handling this.

There are two chapters on instruction. The first (Chapter 5) reviews the context of instruction in a somewhat parallel manner to Chapter 2 on learning. There are, for example, considerable differences in the manner in which instruction is viewed – and this affects the manner in which it is performed, impinging, therefore, on the quality of learning. The second chapter on instruction (Chapter 6) focuses on the ways in which instruction (or the facilitation of learning) best supports the quality of learning that will have impact on practice. It recognizes, however, that the task of the good instructor is not just to enable some of the participants to improve their practice, but to orchestrate the whole group towards this end. The skills of orchestrating improvement in learning in a whole group involve different processes from the support of individual learning. The last section of Chapter 6 looks at some of the technical qualities of good instruction.

Chapter 7 is about the designing of courses to achieve impact. It introduces a flexible framework of areas to address in a short course, which can provide an underpinning for the design of a course. It also introduces the notion of course components. Most textbooks on instruction or training discuss a range of activities that represent the methodology of the instruction. The idea of identifying course components focuses on the role of activities in courses, instead of the activities themselves. Again, here, we are concerned about the precision of course design. The identification of course components in Chapter 7 leads directly into the longest chapter in the book that, in a practical manner, reviews issues raised by each component in turn (Chapter 8).

Chapter 9 can act as a summary of the book, but it acts, in more practical terms, as a 'mind-jog' in the process of course development, when wading through the detail of the full text is inappropriate.

1

The process of building a course – aims, outcomes and their relationship to course impact

Introduction

This chapter concerns elements that are particularly significant for course planning. There will be reference to factors that govern or shape or determine course aims and learning outcomes (structuring factors), and reference to the role, structures and qualities of aims and learning outcomes. There will also be reference to assessment criteria, assessment, the strategy of instruction and the place of evaluation. The structure of a course is important. In a well-designed course there should be discernible relationships between the elements of design – the aim and learning outcomes, the learning outcomes and any form of assessment criteria and thence assessment method.

Aims and learning outcomes are particularly important when the emphasis is on ensuring that courses have an impact, because their presence underpins the precision that is needed to achieve impact. The chapter explores good practice in the writing of clear statements that relate to the quality of the course and to its potential impact and that are more than administrative paper exercises.

Learning outcomes imply the means by which we know that learning has been achieved – ie it implies assessment criteria. While some courses are not assessed, increasingly there is a realization that assessment has different roles. Assessing a course is not just about telling learners how well they know something, but it can be a potent means of improving the impact.

The chapter begins with a review of course development. The section introduces a sequence, which is followed for the rest of the chapter. The start of this sequence is what we have described as structuring factors. Four different factors are identified that may or may not guide the writing of course aims, but they do guide the writing of learning outcomes. The next section looks at the differences between aims, learning outcomes and objectives. Two further sections consider the practical matter of the writing of aims and learning outcomes. There is much to say about learning outcomes: about their content, their uses, and the development of personal learning outcomes by participants on a course. An important point is made about the range of concern of learning outcomes. If there is assessment of the learning, then assessment criteria relate learning outcomes to the assessment task with greater precision; and there are some more general points following this. The final section is completely practical, comprising a list of words that are useful in the writing of learning outcomes and assessment criteria.

Course development

This chapter will follow an 'ideal' sequence of stages for the development of a course. However, ideals are not always followed and a course will not always follow the sequence in the early stages. The sequence starts with the structuring factors that may guide the writing of aims and learning outcomes. Structuring factors are reference points and examples of these are National Vocational Qualifications, professional development frameworks or level descriptors in higher education (HECIW, 1996, Higher Education Credit Initiative, Wales). In the real world a course may be developed in order to relate to one reference point, and later it is mapped on to others.

The sequence of course development that is illustrated below provides a means of checking and improving the coherency of a planned course and hence it promotes good practice. If a course is to be accredited or validated by an external body, then the good demonstration of practice becomes essential. Figure 1.1 provides an overview of the process and the relationships between the elements. It is not a blueprint and the hope is that where it appears to conflict with actual practice, useful thought is stimulated which may or may not in the end concur with the diagram. Structuring factors are described in detail below.

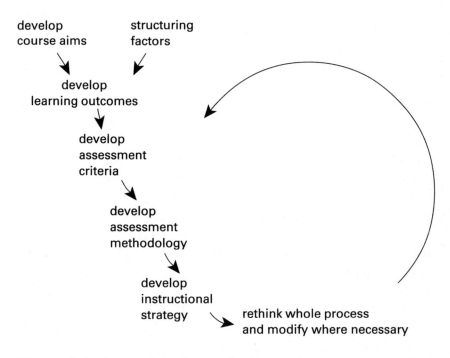

Figure 1.1 *An overview of course development*

Structuring factors that guide the development of a course

Relatively few courses just start up with the writing of aims or learning outcomes. Structuring factors influence the nature, quality or content of the learning that is required in the course and that will be reflected in the manner of setting of aims or the writing of learning outcomes. The most likely factors to influence course design are the following, though several could act together in the same course.

Continuing professional development. Factors that might govern the writing of learning outcomes for short courses are those in frameworks for continuing professional development (CPD). CPD frameworks may determine the types or standards of courses that are deemed appropriate for a particular stage of professional development. They might, for example, require that learners can manage their clients or those with whom they work in a particular but progressively more sophisticated way. The development of a short course to facilitate this learning would be described in learning outcomes that were derived from the framework.

Structuring factors that determine standards. Courses are often offered at different 'levels' or stages. These levels or stages usually relate to the progression of learning and hence reflect increasing complexity of learning. Level descriptors, for example, are statements of the quality of learning that is to be expected of learners at particular stages of higher education (eg HECIW, 1996). Their function is to bring some consistency to the education given in different institutions by providing guidance for writing learning outcomes for modules – and ultimately the function of level descriptors is to provide guidance for standards. Short courses run by institutions of higher education may be described in terms of their 'levels' and learning outcomes for such courses would be written in relationship to a level. There are usually three undergraduate levels and one or more postgraduate levels (eg master's and taught doctorate) (HECIW, 1999). Other courses might be written to support learning for National Vocational Qualifications at different levels.

Curriculum and the desire to inform or share interest. Sometimes – for example in the context of adult education or leisure provision – the curriculum provides the main impetus for the development of a course.

Identified training needs. Here the learner herself or someone else has identified a gap in the learner's functioning. The learner is on the course in order to overcome that gap. It is interesting that a common term for this is 'training need' when in fact the need is for learning and not training. This is a vocabulary issue (see Chapter 2). Training/learning needs are quite different to the schemes mentioned above; they will still govern the development of appropriate learning outcomes. It may be that those determining and describing these 'gaps' should pay more attention to the level of learning that is required. Training or learning needs tend to be described in a manner that does not take account of the depth of learning that is desirable. Later chapters on learning indicate that learning is of different qualities (see Chapter 3).

The relationship of the course to a particular framework may or may not be subject to later evaluation, validation or accreditation.

The differences between aims, learning outcomes and objectives

In this section we consider the distinction between aims, learning outcomes and objectives in order to clarify their roles and to indicate why it may be useful to abandon the term 'objectives'. Aims, learning outcomes and objectives can be written for instruction or learning of any size chunk. They may be written for a single presentation or workshop session, or a day course, or a programme that is made up of many short courses. There is one aim that may be made up of several sub-aims, and there are a number of learning outcomes. The descriptions below relate to a short course. In this context, the term 'learning outcome' refers to the statement of anticipated or intended learning. Unfortunately the words are often used in a generic manner to describe the actual learning that takes place in a course (eg as in Trigwell and Prosser, 1999) where an alternative term might be 'the results of the learning on the course'.

In thinking about aims and learning outcomes, it is important to distinguish between the processes of instructing and those of learning. They are different but clearly their functions are or should be related.

This issue is explored at greater length in Chapter 2. An aim is usually written in terms of a teaching/training or instructional intention. It generally indicates what it is that the instructor is intending to cover in the course, though it may refer to it in terms of the curriculum. In contrast to this, learning outcomes are written in statements of the learning that the learners are anticipated to achieve.

One of the major reasons for confusion in this area of aims, outcomes and objectives lies with the word 'objectives'. Objectives can be written in the form of instructional intentions or in terms of intended learning outcomes. In the same description of a course or part of a course, it is not unusual for both forms of language to be used for objectives. If statements are to be used properly to underpin the structure of a course, learning outcomes, at least, need to be written in the language of learning and not instruction.

Aims

We have suggested that an aim be couched in terms of teaching intention. An example of an aim is given here: 'The aim of this course is to improve the expertise of retail-based pharmacists in helping customers with problems of insomnia.' The statement does not relate to the actual learning process of the participants – who presumably are pharmacists in this example. It is the instructor who will rally resources in order to facilitate the improvement of the expertise. Occasionally words are used that are a little ambiguous. For example: 'The aim is to explore the use of the Internet with infant school children.' Here the aim may be implying that the instructor or the instructor and the learners will do the exploring. The aim could be clearer (who is doing the exploring?). Learning outcomes should also clarify this by indicating the actual learning content for the participants.

If learning outcomes are to be written for a course, the aim can be written as an introductory statement – perhaps more like a rationale. It might describe how the course relates to other courses or mention required prior learning or experience. It may even incorporate some form of mission statement or other generalization about the context of the course. It does not need to be written in one sentence. In the context of Figure 1.1, because an aim is written in terms of teaching or instruction, when the learning behaviour of learners is the central concern of the course, aims are not as directly related to the structuring factors as are learning outcomes. It could be said that they represent the instructor's best guess about how to facilitate the learning that is required. An aim statement may address the quality of the learning that is to be facilitated. It may, for example, suggest that competency is required (Jessup, 1991), or that the learning should be to a certain level or indicate that a general process of informing or education is desired. This can be a helpful element in the aim if it is true for all the anticipated learning, as it then sets a general context.

Learning outcomes

Definition

While an aim is generally about instructing, a learning outcome is about learning. It is an anticipation of what it is that the learner will have learnt at the end of the course and learning outcomes will have a more direct link with structuring factors because the learning is where their influence is expressed. Learning outcomes are inde-pendent of the process of instruction. It is possible for a block of learning to be described only by learning outcomes. This would generally be in the context of independent learning and the learning outcomes indicate to the learner what she will need to learn, usually for some form of assessment process.

Learning outcomes are typically introduced by a phrase such as: 'At the end of the course the learners are expected to be able to…' An example is: '…describe the principles of health promotion as they relate to and might be applied in their practice in nursing. Illustrate them with effective examples.' Or, '…demonstrate in role play three means by which they might introduce suggestions con-cerned with the improvement of health into typical interactions with patients on the ward.'

Sometimes the words used to introduce the outcome statement are 'will be able to'. In a world increasingly keen on litigation, such a statement is potentially dangerous. Those conducting a course cannot ensure that a learner learns, indeed the philosophy of learning that is espoused here emphasizes that the learner is in charge of her learning.

The uses of learning outcome statements

We have indicated that a learning outcome is a statement of the learning that learners are expected to achieve. There are many reasons why it is worthwhile considering the functions that these statements serve. Some of the statements below relate to material above. Some anticipate material that is to follow in this chapter.

- As is suggested above, learning outcomes provide a means of associating the learning on a course with learning needs, or other structuring factors.
- Learning outcomes give direction and purpose to learning or to a course.
- They guide the process of instruction on a course.
- Writing learning outcomes statements provides a principle reference point in the design of a course.
- Learning outcomes make it possible to know when the anticipated learning has been achieved.
- If the course is to be assessed, learning outcomes imply the nature of the evidence of learning that is to be assessed. They may do this through their relationship with assessment criteria that more precisely relate to assessment tasks.
- Learning outcomes are a means of providing information about the learning on the course:
  - to learners who might do the course;
  - to other instructors;
  - to employers;
  - to learners on the course, they help with the planning of learning.
- A record of achieved learning outcomes can provide the text for a transcript of learning (eg for portfolios).
- Learning outcomes help learners to plan their learning.
- Learning outcomes can ensure that the course is designed for focus on impact (see below).

To a large extent, the use that can be made of learning outcomes by the learners depends on the significance attributed to the statements. They may be part of the initial information and never referred to again. At the other extreme, their role in guiding the learning of the participants, and in demonstrating the achievement of that learning as the course progresses or in any assessment procedures, may be considered regularly during the course – perhaps at the beginning of each new topic or on each day. It is only if the latter high profile is given that learners will recognize the statements as reliable and of value. The demonstration of the link of the learning outcomes to the course contents can be a useful manner also of demonstrating the efficiency and effectiveness of the instructor.

Writing learning outcomes

Well-written learning outcome statements have three components. Few people writing a learning outcome would neglect the first two – but few deliberately include the third component. It is mainly the third component that provides the crucial link with assessment criteria and assessment techniques, and also with framework factors that are concerned with standards (such as the level descriptors for higher education or statements from professional bodies). A well-written learning outcome is likely to contain the following components:

- a verb that indicates what the learner is expected to be able to do at the end of the course;
- word(s) that indicate on what or with what the learner is acting – if the outcome is about skills, then the word(s) may describe the way the skill is performed (eg jump up and down *vigorously*);
- word(s) that indicate the nature (in context or in terms of standard) of the performance required as evidence that the learning was achieved.

The components usually follow the sequence above and the statement does not need to be expressed in one sentence. There are some areas of learning in which there is such a clear and understood hierarchy of knowledge – such as in some areas of the physical sciences – that the standard of learning is implied sufficiently in the identification of the subject matter.

The components of a learning outcome are demonstrated in the example given below. The learning outcome is:

> …describe the principles of health promotion as they relate to and might be applied to their practice in nursing. They will be able to provide effective examples of action associated with any principle.

The first component is the verb 'describe'. The action is on the principles of health promotion. The third part is partially expressed as a context (as they relate to and might be applied). Further, the ability to provide effective examples gives an indication of the standard of performance that is expected. This gives a lead to the writing of assessment criteria if there is to be a formal assessment of the course.

There is an important issue about the standard at which learning outcomes are written. Do they apply to the achievements of the excellent learner, the average learner or the learner whose performance sits on the pass/fail line? If learning outcomes are used by learners as a guide for their learning, by implication, the standard of their learning could be inappropriate if they are unclear about the standard to which the learning outcome refers. Most people think that learning outcomes describe the performance of an average learner, but there are many reasons why it is useful that they refer consistently to the minimum acceptable performance. One reason is that this threshold standard provides a baseline that identifies learners whose performance is not adequate. Additionally, it is difficult to define where 'average' performance is located. For example, how much better is it than threshold performance?

One of the comments made in response to the fact that learning outcomes are written at threshold, is that learners will only learn to the minimum standard. That may always be true for some learners. However, assessment that grades above (and below) the threshold can provide the incentive for learners to achieve at higher standards. If there is no assessment procedure, then an alternative incentive is a set of 'desirable learning outcomes'. Either grading or a set of desirable learning outcomes provides a guide to the kind of learning that is required or favoured.

Other than the pass/fail or threshold line, the only other two 'fixed' points in terms of achievement are complete fail and complete success on the learning outcome. The 'complete success' point is, in effect, a statement of competency. The learner either completely passes it or is 'not yet ready' to pass.

The content of learning outcomes

Still recognizing that learning outcomes indicate the learning that is anticipated in the course, there are a few issues worth further consideration. Some advocate the splitting of learning outcomes into different qualities. For example, Pont (1991) suggests (for 'objectives') a division into skills, knowledge and attitudes. Conceptually such division may be difficult at the level of learning outcomes. There are greater opportunities for such fine-tuning when assessment criteria are written (see below).

Because learning outcomes tend to be fairly general statements about learning, it is worth indicating in them the general nature of the learning on the course. This will largely emerge in the verbs (the first component). Strong action words such as 'report' or 'enumerate', 'compare and contrast' tend to give a sense of a course in which learning is factual. Whereas sets of words like 'reflect on and explain', 'summarize', or 'appraise' give a sense of learning through discussion and argument.

Personal learning outcomes

It can be appropriate and valuable to ask course participants to write a set of their own learning outcome statements and to share these with the instructor or with the whole group. This is a manner of discerning the personal orientations of learners to the course (see Chapter 2) and also specific needs or issues that are relevant to the course.

Asking learners to write their own learning outcomes should be well considered first. It may appear to be a laudable and learner-centred initiative, but difficulties can arise. In asking for outcomes to be written, there is a risk that they might not be fulfilled and sore feelings can be thus engendered. A predictable difficulty with personal learning outcomes, is that of enabling the learners to fulfil them when they may require the help of the instructor – and time on a short course is often at a premium. Participants may identify personal learning outcomes that lay well outside the remit of the course. It is important to give a friendly warning that such outcomes may not be fulfilled on this occasion.

Another factor worth considering on a course of several days is the value of asking participants to write their personal learning outcomes at the beginning and at other stages too. If the outcomes that are being produced are being fulfilled within the course, then a session of writing personal learning outcomes at the beginning of each day might be considered.

Learning outcomes and the impact of short courses

There is a point of particular importance to be made about the relationship of learning outcomes to the impact of short courses. Learning outcomes are usually written to refer to the learning achieved at the end of the instruction element of a course – or perhaps where the learning is assessed. However, we have suggested that the ability to demonstrate the learning from the course at the end of the course is not necessarily enough. It is the learning that is involved in changing or improving the workplace practice (or the equivalent) after the course that is significant. This implies that there could be two sets of learning outcomes written for a course – those that refer to learning at the end of the course itself and another set that relates to the changed practice in the workplace. These would be set at an agreed period of time after the course.

The description of the two types of learning outcomes provides a useful challenge to the designers of the course, ensuring that they project their planning to the 'putting into practice' stage. It can be helpful to anticipate the second set of learning outcomes in the first set – perhaps building in notions of transfer of the course learning into the practical situation (Macaulay and Cree, 1999).

We have suggested that it is desirable that learning outcomes relate to some form of assessment procedure. The setting of assessment tasks that concern workplace practice obviously strengthens the commitment and empowers the efforts of both instructors and learners. In some courses it might be appropriate and valuable in terms of learning processes to ask the learners, in consultation with their instructors, to write their own learning outcomes for the workplace practice element of their learning. Additionally they could write assessment criteria for a self-assessment of their new practice.

Another way of looking at the two types of learning outcomes and indeed the course aim, is to consider them as having a range of concern. The course aim is only concerned with the instructor covering what has been specified. The range of concern is very short, and is well under the control of the instructor. The instruction simply has to be done and learning is not at issue. The learner's achievement of the learning outcomes at the end of the period of instruction is at longer range and those written for the workplace practice are at a longer range still, with the control correspondingly less and less.

Assessment criteria and assessment

Assessment may or may not be a part of a short course, though if learning outcomes are written, it could be argued that there should be some means of checking that they have been attained. Until recently, it has not been usual to assess a short course. However, with more concerns about accountability, about the costs versus the benefits of courses within the work context, and with more opportunities for accreditation, assessment is becoming a greater issue (see Chapter 8). If a course is to be assessed there are several contingent decisions. One is whether to assess on the basis of pass/fail or not yet pass – or to give grades. Passing or not passing a course is usually the most important issue and grading can be regarded as a means of enhancing motivation or providing reward for those who achieve above the threshold. On occasions, other factors are contingent on the attainment of a particular grade. In this chapter we are mainly concerned with the place of assessment in determining pass or not pass.

If learning is to be assessed, then the manner of the assessment should be related to the assessment criteria implied in the learning outcome (largely the third part of the learning outcome). Assessment criteria can be thought of as sitting somewhere on a line between learning outcomes and the assessed task. When they are near the learning outcome, they are more generalized and when they are close to the assessment task, they are much more specific, mentioning actual features of the task itself.

There are two types of assessment criteria that correspond with the concern either for passing or failing and for grading. The first type is a threshold assessment criterion. The second type is a grade assessment criterion and this describes the performance that the learner must reach in order to be awarded a particular grade. Threshold assessment criteria and grade criteria coincide at the threshold (on the pass/fail line) only. There are examples of different assessment criteria below. The first example illustrates both the natures of the threshold assessment criterion and the distinction between more general and more specific assessment criteria. The assessment criteria below are derived from the following learning outcome:

> The learner is expected to be able to demonstrate the ability to organize a report of her learning from experience by compiling and presenting a professional portfolio.

A generalized assessment criterion might be the presentation of an effective portfolio showing the organization of her learning from experience. More specific assessment criteria that are closer to the task, but that still relate to the learning outcome, might be:

- The portfolio contains at least six components that are examples of substantial learner experience.
- The portfolio is accompanied by an overarching review of no more than 2000 words.
- The review demonstrates that learning from some components has been applied to others in a considered manner.
- The presentation of the portfolio is well organized, labelled and presented in a professional manner.

The following example is of grade assessment criteria – again for a portfolio:

- Grade A – Outstanding work; the components are well selected and presented. The overarching review shows clear evidence of reflective processes – a result of clearly articulated learning.

- Grade B – Good work: the components of the portfolio have been presented and compiled well. The overarching review shows evidence of reflective processes from which it is evident that some learning has resulted.
- Grade C – This work is sufficiently good to warrant a pass. There are enough components of the portfolio. Presentation is sufficient. The overarching review shows some evidence of reflective processes and some evidence of learning – albeit patchy or disorganized in presentation.
- Grade D – The portfolio is inadequate – being insufficient in size or quality of presentation and/or the overarching review is insufficient in size or quality and/or the quality of the reflective processes is poor or disorganized and there is little or no evidence of new learning. Two or more of these three factors are inadequate.

Some general points about course development

Structuring a programme tightly along the lines described above, using aims, learning outcomes and assessment criteria is often seen as mechanistic, particularly within the context of formal education. Accompanying that is the notion that it 'ties down learning', leaving little freedom for the learner and for the instructor to engage in broader learning and teaching. However, the writing of learning outcomes actually liberates learning. When learning outcomes are written at threshold level, they 'tie down' only the learning that is essential, but leave plenty of opportunity for learning that is above the threshold to be creative or exploratory. Learning outcomes written at threshold say to the learner, in effect, if you learn this material, you will pass the course – almost as a contract.

Alongside the learning outcomes written at threshold, it is possible to write some competency statements – learning that must be mastered perfectly, and some desirable learning outcomes that should be attained at least to a threshold standard of performance (but not perfectly). By being clear about the identity of the learning required, and the appropriate degree of mastery, and where direction is desirable but not essential, it is possible to set up a course with precision and a balance between control and flexibility.

Vocabulary for writing learning outcomes and assessment criteria

Finding the right words for use in writing learning outcomes/ assessment criteria can be difficult, particularly when the statements must mesh with the generic level descriptors. The following list is provided as an aid in this process. The words are organized for convenience under headings that might be seen to accord with those from Bloom's taxonomy (Bloom, 1956). However, no hierarchy is intended. Some words would fit several headings and a child of eight can synthesize a word from a series of letters, so long as the word is not too complex. The words are simply a vocabulary list gleaned from a variety of sources.

Activities giving evidence of knowing

Define, describe, identify, label, list, name, outline, reproduce, recall, select, state, present, be aware of, extract, organize, recount, write, recognize, measure, underline, repeat, relate, know, match.

Activities giving evidence of comprehension

Interpret, translate, estimate, justify, comprehend, convert, clarify, defend, distinguish, explain, extend, generalize, exemplify, give examples of, infer, paraphrase, predict, rewrite, summarize, discuss, perform, report, present, restate, identify, illustrate, indicate, find, select, understand, represent, name, formulate, judge, contrast, translate, classify, express, compare.

Activities giving evidence of knowledge/understanding

Apply, solve, construct, demonstrate, change, compute, discover, manipulate, modify, operate, predict, prepare, produce, relate, show, use, give examples, exemplify, draw (up), select, explain how, find, choose, assess, practise, operate, illustrate, verify.

Activities giving evidence of analysis

Recognize, distinguish between, evaluate, analyse, break down, differentiate, identify, illustrate how, infer, outline, point out, relate, select, separate, divide, subdivide, compare, contrast, justify, resolve, devote, examine, conclude, criticize, question, diagnose, identify, categorize, point out, elucidate.

Activities giving evidence of synthesis

Propose, present, structure, integrate, formulate, teach, develop, combine, compile, compose, create, devise, design, explain, generate, modify, organize, plan, rearrange, reconstruct, relate, reorganize, revise, write, summarize, tell, account for, restate, report, alter, argue, order, select, manage, generalize, précis, derive, conclude, build up, engender, synthesize, put together, suggest, enlarge.

Activities giving evidence of evaluation

Judge, appraise, assess, conclude, compare, contrast, describe how, criticise, discriminate, justify, defend, evaluate, rate, determine, choose, value, question.

2

Learning from short courses: the context of learning

Introduction

Learning, we assume, is the central activity of a short course. In the context of this book, it is assumed that it is not only of central importance that the individual learns on the course, but that she puts her learning into action on return to the workplace. As learning is a central issue, so these three chapters on learning attain particular significance by providing a basis for much of what is written in later chapters.

In this chapter, the word 'context' for learning is interpreted broadly – to include consideration of the way in which the word 'learning' is used and understood as well as the more usual physical interpretations of context in the latter sections. In the next chapter, the focus is on the process of learning and the kinds of learning that can lead to a change in workplace practice. The third of these three chapters on learning concerns the differences between learners that are relevant in short course situations. The chapters on learning provide a basis for consideration of what needs to happen in the process of instruction to facilitate appropriate learning (Chapters 5 and 6).

While learning is central to these chapters, a first task in clarifying its meaning is to separate it from teaching or instruction words. This is the subject matter of the next section in this chapter. A closer view is taken of what is meant and understood by 'learning', and instruction words such as 'teaching' and 'training'. Some of the confusion and lack of clarity in instructing and learning results from a lack of vocabulary. The vocabulary 'gap' is considered and some terms are proposed to fill gaps where this is necessary to the development of this book.

Several sections then address the nature and the perception of learning. This issue may be complicated for the short course situation by the potential range of different learner and instructor perceptions of learning. The following section considers the manner in which views of learning differ in different educational cultures and the effect that these differences could have on the learning in a course. Some of these variations in views of learning are encapsulated in metaphors for learning. Perhaps deepening the confusion for the practitioner trying to understand how learners learn is the range of theories that attempts to explain the process. We do not discuss actual theories, but rather suggest an approach to theories that can make their diversity more manageable.

Two more formal views of learning and knowing are described in the following section. Apart from overtly leisure-oriented courses, most of the learning on short courses comes within the general category of professional learning and knowledge. Eraut's typology of professional knowledge is both simple and helpful (Eraut, 1994). In the subsequent section, one element of his model – experiential learning – is expanded. Somewhat unexplained versions of this form of learning tend to have a central place in the traditional literature of short course learning. The last section in this chapter brings the process of learning in short courses into sharper focus by reviewing some of the issues and constraints that affect learning that occurs in a short course.

Learning and instructing

This section explores both the confusion and the development of clarity in the meanings of learning, and words that imply instruction and the facilitation of learning. The latter words, when clearly distinguished from 'learning' words, will belong with Chapter 5 and 6 (on instruction and the facilitation of learning). This section represents an attempt to cut through the jargon of instruction and learning in order that actions can be clear for both learner and instructor.

The confusion between learning and instruction words

Helping another to learn is different from the action taken by the learner in learning. This may seem obvious, but words for instruction and words for learning are frequently confused in the manner in which they are used. Often the meanings somehow elide. This occurs particularly with the words 'learn' and 'teach'. It is noticeable that young children often confuse the processes of teaching and learning. A child might say, 'I'll learn you to climb that tree' meaning, 'I'll teach you'. Correspondingly, some languages do not distinguish between teaching and learning, having the same word for both (eg Russian). Adults, even those involved in teaching or instruction, are apt to use the words in a manner in which they overlap. In a recent document concerning quality assurance issues in education, a statement suggested that teachers should have particular 'learning intentions' for their students. A teacher can only hope that a student learns – she cannot do it for her. Learning and teaching are separate operations and while learning can be carried out in a separate place from teaching (distance learning), and learning can occur without teaching, teaching or instructing without a learner as object of the activity does not make sense. That instruction or teaching may aim to influence the process of learning in the best possible way is a separate issue that is not in dispute.

The confusion is illustrated in another way when words are applied to learning when they are more to do with the instruction process. For example, Harrison (1991) talks of 'learning events' which encompass 'structured training [and] other approaches through which people can acquire knowledge'. Similarly it is not unusual for activities on courses such as brainstorming, or division into small groups/syndicates, or games and simulations, to be described as learning methods when they are really methods of instruction. In academic education, a lecture or tutorial might often be called a method of learning when, in fact, it is primarily a method by which a teacher instructs or manages the learning of others. The instructor does not know the effect of her instruction on the learner's learning other than by direct questioning or observation. It is not possible to assume that, when confronted with any particular method of instruction, all learners react by learning in the same manner.

Even models of learning may also confuse learning and teaching. The Kolb cycle of experiential learning (Kolb, 1984) is widely used as a means of describing learning, particularly in training situations. In fact it is more often used as a model of the management and facilitation of learning – a teaching model rather than a learning model (Moon, 1999).

It is interesting to muse on why this lack of clarity in instruction and learning words occurs. We have referred already to the differences in culture between the training field and that of teaching and education. The lack of clarity seems more common in the latter, which has a longer history and a stronger identity as a profession. One reason might be the historical developments of a teaching profession in which the action and technical process of teaching is the professional focus – sometimes leaving the learner somewhat to the side.

Another reason for the lack of clarity is that at times there has been a tendency to develop the technology of instruction without deep regard for the impact that it might have on learning. A particular example of this was in the education literature of the 60s and early 70s. In the study of teaching and learning at that time, there was seen to be a very direct link between the activities of instruction and those of learning. Linking instruction and learning in this way focuses on the process of instruction and factors such as the sequence of the ideas presented by the teacher, as a primary influence on the learner's learning.

We provided an example above of one way in which a current and high-profile document confuses teaching and learning. The literature is full of other examples in which there are assumptions that what is taught is learnt or the subject matter of training is learnt without modification other than in memory by the learner. The instructor can only have intentions based on experience and laced (usually) with hopes and faith, and a set of skills in delivery of ideas, of influence and means of facilitation of that learning. The significance of the confusion of instruction and learning is that it leads us to make unwarranted assumptions about the processes and intentions of the learner and therefore it misguides the teacher in her activities. This is an important issue that extends well beyond the running of short courses. It is particularly important in short courses because of the greater need for precision. There is not the time to waste on instruction that does not facilitate learning. The nature of instructing should be clear with a realistic understanding of the impact that it may or may not have on learning.

To this point in this section we have been discussing learning and the words that are summed up in the notion of instruction – which include facilitation of learning, training and teaching. Although this chapter is entitled 'learning', it has been necessary to consider learning in the way that it is commonly viewed and that may involve confusion with the activity of instruction. In order to deal clearly with learning and its various relationships to instruction, the two are better recognized as separate – involving different people doing different things. They can then be brought together again in order to observe with greater clarity the ways in which instruction is or can be related to the learning processes of a learner. In the next section it is convenient to deal with vocabularies associated with both learning and teaching, but thereafter, learning is the central topic for the remainder of this and the next two chapters. Instruction forms the subject matter of Chapters 5 and 6.

Vocabulary issues in learning and teaching

It has been noted that some of the difficulties with understanding the processes of learning and teaching may be due to some missing words in our language. That lack of vocabulary may, in part, explain some of the confusions as well (Moon, 1999 p 104). There is, for example, no word that describes the material that a learner is learning – what she is, in effect, 'taking in'. Correspondingly, since there is also no word for what it is that an instructor conveys or teaches, we are not easily able to articulate that the material that is learnt by the learner is not the same as the material that is produced by the instructor. This perhaps leads to the elision of words for instruction and learning as we have described above. For this book, we use the words **material of learning** for what is learnt by the learner and correspondingly **material of instruction or teaching** for the subject matter of instruction.

Another gap in vocabulary concerns the distinction between the act of learning something and the act of expressing that learning. Most assessment procedures assess both the ability to learn the material and the ability to express that learning in action, in a written response, in an examination, or in fulfilling whatever the task that is set. In many cases the inclusion of both learning and expression of the learning may not matter. Unless learners can express their learning, it is of no value. The issue does matter, however, for a dyslexic person who may have successfully learnt the material of learning, but is unable to represent the learning, for example, in writing. Short courses commonly provide theoretical teaching to underpin practical activities in the workplace. The ability to 'know' how to do something, even to be able to write about it in a task at the end of the course, is of no use if the learner is unable to put the ideas into practice in her workplace. Again as in the previous book, we use the term the **representation of learning** for the expression of that learning either in practice or in an assessed task.

Terms that are particularly useful in the description of learning and teaching processes, but add to vocabulary rather than filling a gap, are **learning challenges** and **teaching challenges**. By this we mean the challenge that a learning task effects for the learner who if facing it and correspondingly the challenge for the instructor (Biggs, 1999 uses the latter term). The same material of learning may pose more or less of a learning challenge to different learners depending on a variety of factors such as prior knowledge and conceptions of the task – as well as how the learner is feeling that day. In a similar way, the same material of teaching and educational situation may or may not pose a greater or lesser challenge to an instructor.

The image of learning

We have suggested that theories of learning tend to incorporate implicit views of the learner. There is plenty of evidence from studies of approaches to learning that the learner's view of learning influences her approach to a learning task and her achievement as a learner (Trigwell and Prosser, 1999). It is also true that theories of instruction have particular views of learning since instructors instruct according to their image of the learner (Trigwell and Prosser, 1999). This section reviews some variations in the image of the learner.

Images of learning in different educational cultures

The learning that occurs in workplace situations may be more instrumental than that in academic education. Learners need knowledge or skills to do a job differently or better and there is often not time or money or particular concern to develop 'the whole person', though there are notable exceptions to this. Instrumentalism is also counteracted in some sectors by the developing ethos of continuing professional development, which is underpinned by a view of personal and professional learning as an interacting system that benefits both the individual and her work. It is interesting to observe the impact that this has on learners' views of their own learning. Among higher education staff, who are now being asked to address their own professional development (NCIHE, National Committee of Inquiry into Higher Education, 1997), a general attitude is that continuing professional development is a timely and appropriate initiative. Nevertheless, in reality, it is often approached as another series of hoops through which they must reluctantly jump in order to preserve their professional status. Their view of their own professional learning may be relatively instrumental after all.

In comparison with academic education, the image of learning in the training field is more often and more comfortably declared to be the guiding activity for instruction. This may suggest that the trainer will go into a training situation ready to be very responsive to the needs of the participants. However, on a short course, it would not be unusual for a trainer to say that she will take account of the needs of the learners – and yet to have in her briefcase a set of notes for the day which she knows she will follow fairly religiously. Handled in a skilled manner, a trainer may listen to the requirements of learners and respond flexibly in a manner that links the requirement back into her intended teaching sequence. Even this scenario does not follow the learner-centredness that some would argue as their philosophy. A learner-centred course with a set curriculum represents an anomaly.

In addition, training can be dominated by methods, techniques and activities that might almost acquire the reputation of being the classic tools of the trade. The PowerPoint presentation, the warm-up activity, the evaluation form, the patterns of seating, and the flip chart and the overhead projector are examples of features that may be presented as if they enhance the power of the learner to learn. They are often, however, more about the enhancement of the power of the instructor or trainer.

The view of the learner in academic education has been subject to a series of different trends over the years. These views may sometimes seem to be secondary to changing views of teaching, which may come from political directions. An obvious example is the change from the progressive education of the 70s and 80s with a holistic view of the learner, towards the more skill/knowledge-focused view of learning that underpins the strengthening of '3Rs' teaching at the beginning of the new millennium. A current example of a changing view of learning within higher education is the notion that learners should know more than purely disciplinary knowledge. In the last few years, there has been perception of a need for graduates to display a range of vocational and social skills. This is influencing the shape of higher education teaching, but also the image of higher education learning.

Another context of learning about which there has been considerable thinking and research is that of adult education. Adults are, of course, involved in both training and academic education and therefore the theoretical orientation could apply equally to the other situations discussed. The field of training has leant, to some extent, on these concepts of adult learning (Zuber-Skerritt, 1992). The distinctiveness of the approach to adult learning rests on the theories of cognitive development. That childhood and adolescence is a period of cognitive development was not questioned, but adulthood was seen as a steady state that lasted until some decline into old age. Educational techniques used with children were applied equally to adults (pedagogy). In the 70s and 80s it was proposed that adult learning could also be subject to development. This led to the adoption of the term 'andragogy' for the education of adults as distinct to children. Andragogy treats adults as possessing relevant experience and personal orientations to and motivations for learning. Adults are viewed as potentially independent and autonomous learners and an implication of the philosophy is that classroom styles of teaching such as lecturing are inappropriate. Discussion or project-based learning is seen as a more appropriate method. Ironically, many adults returning to learning situations are far from independent and suffer considerable uncertainty, often wanting more guidance than younger learners (Usher, 1985).

It seems unlikely that acquisition of the status of adulthood should imply that the learner undergoes a qualitative change in the manner in which she learns. Children and adolescents also possess relevant knowledge prior to most or all learning experiences. The notion of 'adulthood', in itself, is culturally and not physiologically defined. The view that 'adult learning' is only quantitatively different from childhood learning would seem to be an appropriate view (Zuber-Skerritt, 1992). On this basis, learners progress through stages of increasing sophistication in their ability to process intellectual material and it is possible for those who are chronologically adult to be less able to process material than those who are chronologically in childhood or adolescence (Moon, 1999). Such ideas form the basis of discussion later in this chapter. What is important for this section is not, however, the informed ideas that seem to best fit the observed learning of adults and children, but the concepts that are held by those who work in the different sectors of education. If andragogy is seen as different from pedagogy and adult and child learning are perceived to differ, then it is likely that instructors' approaches will differ, perhaps to the detriment of the learning of both groups.

Learner's and instructor's images of learning

It would appear that different educational cultures view the process of learning in characteristic ways. We have suggested that the instructor's view of the process of learning affects the way in which she instructs. Learners also develop a perception of learning either from their educational culture or elsewhere and this will affect the manner in which they learn.

One way in which to elicit perceptions of learning is through metaphor. In many cases, metaphors for learning are associated with metaphors for instructing. Discussion of instruction metaphors will be delayed until Chapter 5. Below, are some metaphors for learning. Some accord with words that will be used in the next chapter to describe depth in learning:

- travelling over a difficult landscape, encountering different terrain;
- swimming, with some swimmers at the surface, some at depth;
- seeing the light;
- making a weaving;
- the building of a brick wall (see next chapter);
- the filling of an empty vessel;
- the putting together of a jigsaw and so on.

In the next chapter metaphor is used in a considerably more sophisti- cated manner to develop a map of learning and the representation of learning based on a constructivist view of learning.

The role of theories of learning

It is not the intention, in this book, to provide detail of a range of theories of learning, but, at the same time, it is important to set a context for the manner in which learning is approached. This brief section has the function of both linking this book to other literature and of distinguishing the approach in this book from much in other literature, particularly the literature on training. Many books on training and running short courses contain a chapter on learning and, as in this book, that view of learning is often implied to be central to the manner in which the book concerned describes the process of training.

While there are many accounts of learning in the literature, there are few that help the reader to understand how the approaches relate to each other. Many books, particularly in the training field, provide their own account as if that explains all that is necessary to know about learning. We have mentioned the use of the Kolb cycle as a widespread means of explaining learning (Kolb, 1984). The result of the presentation of a single viewpoint is that readers either have a very simplistic view of learning or they are confused. They might either let that bother them or live with it, coping perhaps by not thinking too much more about the mysterious process of learning that is now made more mysterious by the different attempts to describe it. The anomaly becomes even more uneasy when one crosses the cultural boundaries between training literature and that from formal education and educational psychology, which can demonstrate an even wider diversity of accounts of learning.

The general position held in this book, is that is that no one theory provides all that we need to know about learning. It is also probably true to say that theories are rarely devoid of some explanatory or descriptive value even if sometimes that has more to do with the manner in which it directs the activities of instruction rather than explaining learning. It is also necessary to be able to take what is useful from some theories and to feel free to disregard those that do not have as much to offer at the time, bearing in mind that they may support understanding at a later stage or in a different context. It is important also to note that any theory of learning has in it an implicit view of the learner (Zuber–Skerritt, 1992) and it is for this reason there is some exploration of different views of learning in these chapters.

We have described constructivism as a core idea in this book (eg Marton, Hounsell and Entwistle, 1997). We have said that the ideas of Kolb, on experiential learning, are commonly cited in the literature of training and short course learning. Though frequently rejected, behaviourism provides valuable ideas about encouraging learning through positive reinforcement (Pithers, 1998). The work of those interested in accelerated learning focuses on the conditions that are seen as enhancing the abilities for learning in the brain beyond those usually exploited (eg Rose, 1985).

The subject matter of learning and knowing

The use of terms such as 'learning', 'knowing', 'understanding', and so on, begs questions about their definition. The definition of such words is, in effect, the subject matter of the next two chapters. To start with, however, we take learning to be the action by an individual, of taking in ideas in order to know or understand them, or in order to represent the learning alone or in combination with other ideas in some form of expression. At a later stage we will distinguish between knowing and understanding but for the present, knowing/ understanding is taken to mean the ability to represent ideas that have been learnt either in their original form or in an interpreted form. A difficulty in definition that has been mentioned before is that we cannot know that an individual has learnt or knows something except through the medium of the representation of the learning/knowing – and it is useful to recognize this as a separate action.

A typology of professional knowledge – Eraut's model

Many short courses, particularly where impact is an issue, are set in the context of professional development. One short course might be on an improvement of management skills, another on applying the theory of health promotion within the context of teaching. Another course might be on forklift truck handling skills or hedge laying, another may be improving problem-solving skills, another on becoming more assertive and another may be on improvement of training skills. The kinds of knowledge involved in these short courses differ. Some involve more learning about theory, while some are more concerned with skills. Some involve the development of personal behaviour which, in turn, is applied in a work situation (assertiveness and management). Eraut has produced a 'map of professional knowledge' that enables these different forms of learning to be seen in relationship to one another (Eraut, 1994). This 'map' provides a useful reference point for discussion of the subject matter of short courses.

Eraut describes propositional knowledge as including the usual material taught on initial professional development courses. It is represented by espoused or disciplinary theory, ideas that are derived and generalized from relevant applied fields of professional practice and from specific instances in the discipline. This is the material that characterizes the discipline but which tends to become dated. It has been assumed that professionals rely on this knowledge as the source of theory from which they derive their professional skills in practice. Schön (1983) suggests that we retain the illusion that only propositional knowledge guides practice but, in fact, 'on the job' learning builds 'theory-in-use' that itself becomes important as a guide for practice.

Eraut's second form of professional knowledge is personal knowledge, the accumulated 'impressions, personal knowledge and the interpretation of experience' (Eraut, 1994 p 104). This is theory-in-use, the ideas, the smaller and larger experiences in the work situation, that guide future practice. Some of this material may be generalizable, almost assuming the status of propositional knowledge, but much remains at the level of impression and is relatively unorganized and tacit.

In terms of professional development courses, this means that the traditional structure of many, particularly in the academic context, can be inappropriate for the purposes of professional development (Schön, 1983, 1987). The traditional academic view of knowledge tends to be that practice follows theory. This may be true where the profession concerns many instrumental activities and direct application of knowledge such as in engineering and medicine. However, the discussion above suggests that in other professions, theory may guide initial ideas in practice, but very soon the practitioners are developing theories-in-use and making less reference to espoused theory. That practitioners have difficulty in elucidating what guides their practice tends to reinforce their belief that it is still propositional knowledge that remains their guide to practice. Moon suggests that in a situation where they are challenged for the explanation, they are more likely to 'reach for' their recollections of espoused theory (Moon, 1999, pp 52–53).

In a formal learning situation such as a short course, emphasis on propositional knowledge can distort practical learning when an instructor does not recognize or is not able to work with the shift to 'theory-in-use'. Personal knowledge plays an important part in placing an emphasis on the current practice with regard to the subject matter of the course (see Chapter 7). The developing literature on reflection, and the rhetoric of 'the reflective practitioner', demonstrate an increasing acknowledgement of the role of personal knowledge in professional or workplace activity.

The third type of knowledge described by Eraut is process knowledge. This consists of five kinds of process – 'acquiring information; skilled behaviour; deliberative processes, eg planning and decision-making; giving information; and metaprocesses for directing and controlling one's own behaviour' (p 107). These processes tend to characterize the profession either in the kind of action involved in the skilled behaviour or in the cognitive processes and discourses involved, for example, in the non-physical skills. This form of knowledge would be the subject matter of many more practically-oriented short courses.

Different professions will demand different emphases on the forms of professional knowledge. Some will focus on process knowledge; some will rely more on propositional knowledge than personal knowledge, and some vice versa. Taylor (1997) suggests that it will be the professions, such as teaching and social work, which deal with the unpredictable behaviour of people, that will rely more on personal knowledge than professions such as engineering that have more sound guidance from established theory. Later in this chapter there is reference to the importance of short courses in providing 'intellectual space' to allow participants time in which to reflect on and process the 'impressions' amassed in practice.

Learning from experience

'Experience' is a fundamental source of personal knowledge (see above). We expand on this aspect of personal knowledge – that of 'impressions, personal knowledge and the interpretation of experience' (Eraut, 1994) – because it has become so significant in the literature, particularly that of training and adult education. Many accounts of learning in short courses suggest that learning from experience is the only manner in which adults learn and the Kolb cycle of experiential learning is presented as the manner in which this learning occurs (eg Sheal, 1989).

What is the meaning of the word 'experience' in the context of learning? Most references to experiential learning imply the involvement of psychomotor action and this has come to support a belief that learning is achieved more effectively if something active is 'done'. Later, more discussion of learning (Chapter 3, p 79) indicates that there are good reasons for such a belief, but the belief is probably too generalized and attains the status of a myth about adult learning, and action tends to be one of the theoretical tenets of adult education (andragogy). The picture is complicated when learning from 'experience' may be said to include attending and learning from interaction in a lecture situation. The stream of information in such a context may provoke questions in the listener's mind, but may or may not leave them unresolved because the opportunity for response or resolution is not provided (see Cunningham, 1983 and Steinaker and Bell, 1979 also include vicarious learning as a form of 'experiential learning').

Eraut addresses the problem of defining experiential learning. He says:

> To avoid the truism that all learning is experiential…I propose to restrict the term 'experiential learning' to situations where experience is initially apprehended at the level of impressions, thus requiring a further period of reflective thinking before it is either assimilated into existing schemes of experience or induces those schemes to change in order to accommodate to it' (Eraut, 1994).

It is interesting to note that this definition says nothing about 'learning by doing' in a psychomotor sense. The 'doing' is the brain work. However, the notion of learning by doing is strong, significantly among those who are the potential learners. Recognizing the confusion about the definition of experiential learning, Burnard asked his nursing students what they understood by experiential learning (Burnard, 1991). For them, experiential learning was any learning that occurred outside of a classroom. On this basis there is a question about the status of a demonstration of a nursing procedure carried out both in and outside the classroom. The thinking of the nursing students is probably no more confused than that common in the literature that underpins much short course instruction.

We have referred several times to the Kolb cycle of experiential learning (Kolb, 1994). It has been applied widely in many situations but it has been reinterpreted by many writers and sometimes the use of different words means that it does not look a like the original version. Kolb starts with a learner being involved in an experience – the notion of 'concrete experiencing'. In order to enable the learning to proceed, the experience is subjected to 'reflective observation'. Kolb does not say much about what he means by reflection or reflective observation, but this process leads into another process of 'abstract conceptualization'. Writers often interpret abstract conceptualization as the 'learning' process, though for others, learning is the whole cycle. The material of learning is subjected to 'active experimentation' – it is put into action or tested in some way. The action creates a new experience from which the learner can again learn – and the cycle revolves – though possibly not always in that sequence of events. Some of these interpretations are easier if, as we have suggested earlier, the cycle is mainly viewed as one of the management of learning rather than learning itself.

Features of the learning process that are valuably emphasized in the Kolb cycle are that the learning perpetuates itself and that in moving through the cycle, the learner shifts her role from actor to observer – from 'specific involvement to general analytic detachment'. The 'analytic detachment' provides a significant role for reflective activity that is ignored in many other theories of learning.

With reference to the changing roles of the learner in the process, Kolb suggested that particular capacities might be required in different phases of the model. Further development of this led to the idea that learners might have preferred styles of learning that make them more effective in one or more phases than the other sectors of the cycle. The work on learning styles has been widely cited, particularly in the field of training, and it will be mentioned briefly with reference to the factors in the learner (Chapter 4).

We have said that the Kolb cycle has been influential. However, the high esteem in which it tends to be held in the training and adult education fields can provide something of a contradictory situation for those who run short courses. It can result in the over-emphasis of learning from (active) experience. Learning from experience, whether the experience is cognitive or physical, takes longer than learning from material that is more processed – and short courses are short. However, theoretical learning will need to be reinterpreted by the learner into action in her workplace and the lack of this reinterpretation phase may be a reason why some courses fail to have an impact. The decision as to the appropriateness of an experiential or more pre-processed approach to the material is likely to be a matter of a cost-benefit sum, playing off the quality of learning required against time/cost factors.

The value of the Kolb cycle might be that it provides a structure for the process of learning – or does it, perhaps, impose a structure on the process of instruction? It is to organize a sequence of instruction that the cycle is most frequently used. On this basis, it is important that the sequence is appropriate. Moon (1999) argues that reflection is a process that occurs after the learning of something. It is secondary and a form of 'rethinking' – a form of cognitive reorganizing and perhaps recategorizing and not a part of the initial process of learning from involvement in experience. The consequence of this matters in the structuring of short courses if the cycle is used by an instructor to guide learning (ie in an instructional context). Such guidance will direct the learner to reflect in order to learn, when the learner might prefer to learn and then reflect on how the learning relates to what she knows. This possible reversal might apply particularly in the situation where the learning is from raw experience. On later 'cycles', where the reflection is on the experimentation with learning and some learning has already been accomplished, the sequence matters less. Indeed, Kolb somewhat vaguely suggests that the events may happen in different orders – it is those who interpret his work who adhere more closely to the sequence.

The environment of learning

Earlier sections in this chapter have been concerned with the context of learning in terms of the interpretation of the word. This section is concerned with the setting in which learning occurs. The first part provides an overview and a constructivist perspective on the influence of the environment on the learner through a systems approach (Biggs, 1999). Within the context of that approach the concept of limiting factors is introduced. The approach and the ideas that accompany it will inform the subsequent chapters, especially the next two.

A systems approach to learning means that the environment is viewed as anything that might influence the learner's learning. In other words, it includes the immediate physical environment, the ethos of the relevant organization or institution, the instructors and the process of instruction, the social environment, and the effects of the weather outside, and so on.

Biggs applies his thinking particularly to higher education and uses the notions of micro-systems and macro-systems. The micro-system includes the factors that are immediate and impinge directly on the learner. In terms of a short course, this would include the factors that directly influence learning such as physical and social situations, that of the instruction. It would include factors at an organizational or institutional level such as organizational culture, policies that affect, for example, the numbers admitted to a short course. It could include the strategies for support of implementation of the learning, the level of support for those who want to further their learning, and so on. Oates and Watson (1996) identify some of the macro-system factors that operate in a higher education environment. The macro-system often operates through the micro-system.

The systems that impinge on a learner are mapped by Biggs as a series of concentric circles with the learner in the centre. These increase in diameter as the influence on the learner fades. The teacher is in the second circle, and what Biggs describes as the teaching context is in the third. The outer circle, which may still be relevant to a short course, is the community and variables such as political pressures.

On the basis of a constructivist approach to the learner's environment, the learner constructs her view of the environment and responds to external factors on the basis of a unique pattern of knowledge and understanding (cognitive structure – see p 65) or of patterns of reaction. This means that constant music in an environment, for example, might be disruptive to one learner, but might enhance the performance of another. Similarly, hand drawing on overhead slides might be welcomed as a more personal approach by one learner and perceived as 'unprofessional' by another. The presence of a 'welcome' notice in glue and glitter might be attractive to some, and flippant or patronizing to others (Lawlor and Handley, 1996). What actually affects the learner in an environment, is what she perceives or is prone to respond to and the manner in which she perceives it or responds. In this way the contents of learning environments, like any other environments, are therefore unpredictable and limitless. That, however, may be taking matters too far. It does not help an instructor in the development of an environment that is conducive to learning if the only source of information on that basis is the learners. Neither is it possible to cater for every single learner, nor are the individual preferences of learners evident before a course.

To accommodate subjective and objective views of the environment, Trigwell and Prosser use two terms. They talk of the learning context which is the objective setting in which learning occurs – the course, the instructor, relevant organizations, and so on – and the learning situation, which is the learner's perception of the context and unique to the learner. They suggest that a learning situation uniquely 'evokes certain prior experiences of learning, perceptions of the present context and approaches to learning in that context' (Trigwell and Prosser, 1999, p 74). In the context of a short course, the important part of one learner's situation might be the quality of the instruction, but for another it might be the presence of biscuits with the afternoon tea, and somehow these anomalies have to be accommodated or modified.

Another fundamental issue in the consideration of the environment of learning is the ways in which environmental factors interact. The notion of a 'system' implies that the learning environment is to be viewed in a holistic manner – as would be appropriate for any ecological system in the natural environment. It also implies operation of a process whereby every action works towards a state of equilibrium. For example, a learner on a short course has decided that her interest in the course is the day away from work, and does her best to achieve her end, but has to resist the influences of her colleagues who are there because they want to change their work practice. The instructor spends time and effort trying to motivate the learner in order to perform her own role in a satisfactory manner. However, in so doing, she affects the way in which she is perceived by others. The change in one element in an equilibrium affects others since all constantly seek equilibrium.

If the learning environment is, or operates in the same manner as, an ecosystem, then there are useful principles that apply to both. One is the principle of limiting factors (Odum, 1968). Originally, the concept of a limiting factor arose in the descriptions of how nutrients affect the survival of plants in an ecosystem. The idea was then applied more broadly to any factor in a system. The presence and success of organisms in an environment depends on a range of conditions. For plants, as well as nutrients there would be light, water, temperature, carbon dioxide in the atmosphere and space for roots, and so on. A factor (or condition) becomes a limiting factor when it is at the limit of tolerance for the organism. If a plant fails while the supply of nutrients (or more likely, a particular nutrient) drops while other conditions remain the same, the nutrient at that level of concentration is a limiting factor.

Such an idea has wide application in the field of psychology and education. In the current context of learning on short courses, an example might be of a participant in a course, who should be an effective learner, but finds the room in which the short course is run very claustrophobic so that her state affects her ability to learn. The state of being upset is a limiting factor to her learning.

In terms of learning, then, a limiting factor might be defined in the following way:

> the success of learning depends on a complex of conditions, so that any condition that approaches or succeeds a particular tolerance so as to limit the quality of the learning , is the limiting factor in that situation (Moon, 1999 after the ecological definition of limiting factors in Odum, 1968).

In ecology, the definition of limiting factors is developed to include the idea of 'factor interaction'. This idea suggests that the effects of a limiting factor may be mollified by the action of another agent. Therefore, the presence of other substances in the soil can allow the plant to be more tolerant of the effect of a limiting factor. In terms of the example for learning, a talk with another participant might make the learner more able to tolerate the limiting factor and her learning improves.

On the basis of these influences on learning, it is possible to consider that the environment shapes learning (Eizenberg, 1988), but the relevant environment is that which is perceived by the learner, which may not be the same as the environment judged to be affecting her by another. The effect on learning is usually expressed through the approach that the learner adopts to her learning (see next chapter). The principle of constructivism and the interactions of factors in the environment can be applied to the situation of the instructor as much as it can apply to that of the learner.

The social environment and learning

An important aspect of the environment of the learner is the social context, and more specifically the other participants on the course. There are plenty of publications on learning in groups (eg Jaques, 1991) but very often the focus is on the management of groups in terms of shapes and sizes and interaction patterns, rather than the concern for whatever advantages there might be from working in that manner. What is it that a learner gains from learning in a social situation rather than alone and because of that, what aspects of the social context of learning should be developed?

Reviewing the literature on the advantages of small group teaching, Brown and Atkins summarize recent work and conclude that: 'small group teaching is usually better than other methods at promoting intellectual skills including problem-solving and at changing attitudes, and about as effective as other methods at presenting information…its potential lies in the interplay of ideas and views that develop a (learner's) capacity to think' (Brown and Atkins, 1997, p 52).

In other words, it is fairly obvious to conclude that there appears to be nothing special to be gained from instructing in a group situation unless there is the opportunity for learners to interact with each other and to learn from the interaction. Indeed, working in a group might be construed as disadvantageous compared with working in a one-to-one relationship with a tutor (eg coaching) since the individual attention is diluted. Sometimes this process of interaction occurs at meal breaks or, if the course is residential, at the end of the day. It is for this reason that breaks in a short course are considered as part of it when we look at 'components' in Chapter 8.

There are many reasons why social interaction can play an important part either in facilitating learning or in reinforcing learning. Some of the reasons relate to sections in the next few chapters, and references are given accordingly. Some relate directly to learning and some relate indirectly to learning (towards the end of the list).

- Social interaction implies that learners talk about a topic. Talking is a form of representing learning and, as such, it will reinforce and sometimes deepen learning.
- Talking about a topic enables learners to check their understanding. They receive feedback on the understanding that they display (Abercrombie, 1979).
- There may be a requirement for the learners to go beyond talking, to explain or present their views or to discuss a product of reflection on a topic. In these cases, the learning is deepened.
- Learning from discussion can be challenging. It can be an example of 'messy' learning and we suggest in Chapter 4 that this kind of learning is necessary in professional development.
- Some on the course may know more than others or be more sophisticated in their thinking. They are then a learning resource (Taylor, 1997).
- Social interaction within a group of learners who have a discipline or profession in common reinforces process knowledge (Eraut, 1994). It enables learners to recognize and become more proficient in the relevant discourse (Brown and Atkins, 1997).
- Social interaction in the form of group contributions to knowledge may be the focus for the major elements of learning on a course. Quite often the required expertise is present within the group of participants and the role of the instructor is to enable learning to be generated, recognized, processed and relearnt in an appropriate manner.
- Exploiting social interaction is a useful method for the instructor of regaining attention by changing pace and activity. Moving into an interactive situation usually means that some people move physically.

- Social interaction on a course can enable participants to be more willing to be open to new ideas and changes of attitude.
- More viewpoints or ideas arise in a group than usually is the case in an individual (eg in brainstorming).
- Social interaction usually increases the enjoyment of the course.
- Where other participants are unsure of their knowledge or understanding, they find it easier to check with peers rather than with the instructor.
- There may be a subtle therapy or support role played by a group for individuals.

Some of the social interaction described above, will occur spontaneously in a group when the instruction stops (eg coffee time), but for many of the situations mentioned, it will be necessary for the instructor to design the process so that the interaction is focused in the manner that she plans. This will apply, in particular, to situations where learners find it easier to check with peers rather than with the instructor. The purpose of learning with others is to deepen learning or challenge existing thinking.

A mistake is often made in assuming that learners, who do not necessarily know each other, will automatically engage in group work without any preparation. Much has been written of the stages of group formation, and the progress through these stages will be working in parallel with the developing role of the group as an environment for learning. The processes can conflict where group 'roles' – such as leader or expert – interfere with the agenda for learning, where, for example, one person with an agenda for dominating the group does not listen and respond to others. There is often heavy encouragement towards group activities in short courses in the literature and it is important to stress that learning to function in a group and learning from being in a group may be useful learning, but it does not need to be a part of every course.

The context for learning on a short course

A short course is a particular context or environment in which learning takes place and there are points worth making about the manner in which this might affect the process of learning itself. In this section we apply more specifically material from earlier in this chapter, and in most cases there will be a return to the points made below at later stages in the book.

We have suggested that there are different **views of learning in different educational cultures** and that a learner's view of learning is likely to affect her approach to a learning task. The expectations associated with experiences of other short courses will be compounded with expectations of this course (eg developed from precourse literature, and so on) as well as the actual experiences on the course, which will include the nature and approach to instruction. We have mentioned that there is a range of techniques that has become particularly associated with short course situations such as 'snappy' presentations, 'warm-ups', brainstorming, small group work leading into plenary 'report back' sessions. In contrast, most short courses do not contain traditional lectures, one-to-one seminars or homework of essays to write.

A feature of the learning in short courses that is central to the theme of this book is that it is **learning that should have impact on practice**. However, the contrast should be made between learning in short courses that requires to be put into practice the following day, and the kind of learning in many academic programmes where the ideas may or may not ever directly influence work practice. Relatively few students, for example, work in situations that match the subject matter of their degrees. Learners new to the experience of short courses may find them to contrast considerably with previous experiences of learning.

The length of the course is significant. **A short course is short**. There may be too much to cover in the time allocated – perhaps because of poor judgement, or perhaps it is because the tendency of the course managers or teachers to be over-optimistic or overenthusiastic. In line with the above comments about the confusion and elision of the processes of teaching and learning, there may be an assumption that more teaching will automatically mean more learning. Sometimes it means that there is learning but of a lesser quality (Trigwell and Prosser, 1999, p 159).

In short courses **learning is usually concentrated** and not dispersed, with a number of subject areas being presented at the same time. This is another different pattern from that in most formal education situations, though learners in a physics class in higher education were given their course in a concentrated form rather than the usual dispersed presentation and many preferred to learn in this way (Parlett and King, 1971). Some of the reasons for the preference were for the social opportunities. Concentrated learning may well be among the helpful characteristics of the short course.

Another consideration about short course learning that is linked to the short length is that of **intellectual space** (Barnett, 1997). This is a time for reflection. There are at least two aspects to this. The first is straightforward: when time is short and teaching is concentrated, there may not be sufficient time given to the learners to reflect on and thus to consolidate their learning (Moon, 1999). The second is an observation that the value of many short courses to the participants is that they provide time to reflect on their work practices, sometimes just those experiences relevant to the course, and sometimes more generally. This relates back to the discussion of Eraut's map of professional development earlier in this chapter. We suggested that personal knowledge guides much practice, but that it tends to be tacit. On the assumption that an instructor is aware of this and is not inappropriately stressing propositional knowledge, intellectual space provides an important opportunity for a review of the personal knowledge that is relevant to the material of learning on the course. This is an important issue in course design and it is discussed at greater length, with reference to the framework to improve the impact of short courses, in Chapter 7.

'**Tidy**' or '**messy**' may seem to be strange words to use in the description of learning, but they have proved to be useful in considering the role of reflection in learning (Moon, 1999, 1999a). They allow us to consider more characteristics of learning in short courses. Where time is short, it may be desirable to reduce the learning challenge that is presented to learners. This may mean, for example, that the material of teaching is – to use a metaphor – processed and packaged supposedly to facilitate easy learning. While the learning may be easy, it may then need to be applied in complex situations – the swampy grounds of professional functioning as described by Schön (1987) – which could then be a considerably greater challenge for the learner. Making learning 'easy' does not mean that it will be 'easy' to apply in a complex situation. It is interesting to note the recognition of this problem in medical/dental courses of a few years ago and the commonly practised solution of raising the learning challenge by using a problem–solving basis for many courses (eg Wetherell and Mullins, 1996). In contrast to this deliberate effort to make learning more realistically 'messy', learning in formal higher education has tended to become 'tidier' as student numbers have increased and it has become easier to provide more material on handouts or to put lecture notes on computer networks. Learning is a 'messy' process and it may be that learners should not too often be too protected from the confrontation with this characteristic (King and Kitchener, 1994).

3

Learning from short courses: depth and meaning in learning

Introduction

In any educational situation, it is important to understand the quality of the learning that is required in order that the course can be suitably designed. Sometimes there is a need simply to learn facts and be able to reiterate them on demand. An example might be the learning of licensing laws concerning under-age drinking. In situations where the impact of the learning on a practice situation is important, the learning will need to be at a deeper level. An example is the understanding of how to handle a situation in which under-age people want to purchase alcoholic drink.

The issue of the depth of the learning that is needed by a learner is not widely discussed in the context of training or short courses. One reason is that the required depth may be indicated to learners only implicitly in the context of assessment tasks. However, in short courses there may be no assessment tasks. Another way that required depth of learning could be signalled is in the learning outcomes for a course. Signals about depth may emerge in the distinction between such words as knowing and understanding and in the distinction that is made between rote learning and the learning that is sufficiently coherent that the learner can explain it to another. The issue is more generally approached in the material on student learning that defines deep and surface learning.

The sequence of models and ideas that are included in this chapter is designed progressively to build a picture of stages of learning which will, in turn, underpin a map of learning and the representation of learning towards the end of the chapter. The chapter begins with several descriptions of learning in which distinctions between deeper or more complex and less deep forms of learning are made. These informal discussions of the qualities of learning lead into discussion of the work on approaches to learning and the distinction between deep and surface learning matches. The next section takes forward the constructivist notions of learning and links this to the idea that learning is the process of development and modification of a cognitive structure. The development of a 'map of learning and the representation of learning' places the functioning of the cognitive structure in relation to a series of stages of learning that accord with deep and surface qualities of learning and different qualities of the outcomes of learning. The suggested nature of these stages of learning is presented on pp 71–75 and the 'map' suggests ways in which the learning might be deepened. The last section elaborates on some implications of the 'map' for learning in short courses – focusing on reflection and further aspects of experiential learning.

Quality in learning and the representation of learning

Knowing and understanding

Berman–Brown (1994) provides some useful, though not completely consistent, distinctions between the notion of knowledge and understanding. While knowledge can be obtained through experience, understanding requires a grounding of knowledge and suggests a deepening of or reflection on that knowledge. It implies a knowing of 'the origins and the context' (p 323) of something. Knowledge can be developed by memorizing, but this memorizing would not enable understanding. He suggests that generally knowledge is associated with ideas of truth and implies possession of 'a range of information'.

Schuck provides a useful description of different depths of learning in the context of a workplace in which workers are learning to use new technology. She talks of the learning needs that might emerge with the process of automation in a company:

> ...learning is typically concerned with 'computer literacy' – a working knowledge of how the computer system operates, general ways in which it can be used, and basic keyboard skills. The worker visualises *objects* (such as pieces of equipment or the steps in the process) and translates this concrete reality into numbers on the terminal screen and memorises actions, the standard operating procedures necessary to perform the job through the terminal. Performance is evaluated on the basis of how well the worker has learned objects and actions, but he or she may not understand or be able to articulate the underlying rationale or meaning of the task.
>
> (Schuck, 1996, p 201)

Schuck suggests that there is a second stage in the process of learning 'if information is to be dealt with in any significant way' (p 201). The worker needs to progress from working with objects and actions to working with meaning, moving from a 'preprogrammed way (If X happens, I do Y)' (p 201), to a situation in which she understands how one event affects another. She cites the words of one worker who recognized this change in his learning: 'When I used to look at the numbers, I could see the process. But now the numbers talk to me'. Schuck comments, '"The numbers talk" when workers make them mean something'. When this meaning is present, workers can 'make conscious and intelligent choices to solve problems or to identify more efficient or effective approaches to the business' (p 201). She argues the importance of a training that teaches people not only 'what to think', but 'how to think' (p 204).

Coherence and complexity of learning

Learning 'how to think' involves more than deepening the capacity to understand at one level of complexity of material. It involves learning from material of greater complexity and the development of greater ability to represent that learning in a coherent manner.

Some work that started in Australia a couple of decades ago makes generalizations about the quality of the representation of learning as a means of making deductions about the quality of the learning that preceded it. The SOLO taxonomy (Biggs and Collis, 1982) appears to provide a means of describing the ability to deal with depth and complexity of learning through observation of its representation. SOLO stands for Structure of Observed Learning Outcomes. Biggs (1999) suggests that it '...provides a systematic way of describing how a learner's performance has grown in complexity' (p 37). It is relatively simple and has many uses in conceptual and practical situations. The five levels of representation in SOLO demonstrate the increasing demand for coherence and holistic understanding of the learning task. The taxonomy provides a useful framework for application to Schuck's description of the stages of learning in the workplace (above). More significantly, it relates to the ideas of surface and deep learning to which reference is made later in this chapter.

The levels are described below, using quotations from Biggs (1999, pp 38–39) as illustration. For convenience it is described here in terms of the written work of learners, though it can be used for other forms of representation (eg to determine classes of a degree):

- The first, the **prestructural** level, is represented by words that demonstrate little understanding of the topic that is to be discussed. 'The point is missed.'
- The second level, the **unistructural** level, is represented by writing that follows one aspect of meaning but demonstrates no broader understanding of the topic – learners 'get on track but nothing more'.
- The **multistructural** level representations tend to contain a range of relevant facts, but they are not logically related in order to provide a deeper picture of the meaning that could be elicited. It is as if the learner can '...see the trees but not the wood. Seeing the trees is a necessary preliminary to adequate understanding, but it should not be interpreted as comprehending the wood.'
- On the basis of the metaphor, the fourth level, **the relational** level, begins to address the wood. Learners demonstrate comprehension of the point of their writing and sense is made of the

topic as a whole.'This is the first level at which "understanding" in an academically relevant sense may be appropriately used.'

● The **extended abstract** level might often go beyond the level of work expected. It may be applied or generalized in new contexts and to new subject matter and represents new knowledge to the learner.

A criticism of the taxonomy is that the nature of the representations of learning might be accounted for not only by the learning but also by the content of the material itself. For example, the structure of a task to be assessed might steer the response of the learner towards a particular level, rather than encourage the display of the quality of the best learning.

On the basis of the SOLO taxonomy, Schuck's workers represent their learning in their actions on the keyboard through which they achieve their objectives. They start at prestructural or at the uni-structural state – key by key or 'on track', but operating with no broader understanding than how the pressing of one button causes an anticipated action. It would seem that those to whom 'numbers talk' have moved to the relational level. They are able to make sense of the data and to use it to operate in ways that are more under their control because they understand the implications of their actions.

Deep and surface approaches to learning

While in some senses this section is a discussion of another perception of the qualities of learning, the concept of deep and surface approach can explain the previously discussed qualities. This discussion has great significance for the remainder of the book. The original ideas were developed in Sweden in the 1970s and they provided a new way of considering learning. Much learning research had consisted of varying the conditions around learning – such as environmental factors or the quality of instruction, while measuring the success of the learners. This phenomenographic research initially consisted of giving learners a reading-for-learning task and asking them how they conceived of the learning that they considered was required and the approach that this led them to take to the task. The learners who approached reading in order to elicit the meaning of the material took what was termed a deep approach. Others tried to memorize aspects of the text without trying to understand its meaning and correspondingly they were seen as taking a surface approach (Marton and Saljo, 1997). Descriptions of deep and surface approaches to learning follow.

Surface approach

The general intention of the learner tackling material of learning is to memorize or know as much of the content as it is necessary to know. The learner does this by memorizing material in a routine manner without reflecting on it or the underpinning purposes or structure of it or relating it to previous learning or knowledge. Elements that may have a logical relationship are treated as if unrelated if the material appears easier to learn in this manner. A consequence of this is that the learner has difficulty in making sense of ideas. The learner is not likely to show interest in the material and may come to feel anxious and under pressure if she feels that she is not learning properly. This is a vicious circle since learners are also more likely to adopt a surface learning approach when they feel under pressure – for example before assessment.

Deep approach

A deep approach to material of learning, in contrast, is where the learner has an orientation towards seeking the meaning in the material and understanding the ideas in it. She is likely to be an interested learner, observing underpinning principles, patterns, and the structure of the material, relating it to previous knowledge and understandings, critically examining or questioning the logic and argument in the material. It appears to be harder to sustain this approach when learners are anxious or under pressure in their learning situations. (After Entwistle, 1996.)

Entwistle (1988) illustrates the approaches from studies of students reading an article. Those who adopted a surface approach had the intention to 'memorize those parts of the article that they considered important in view of the questions they anticipated afterwards. Their focus of attention was thus limited to the specific facts or pieces of disconnected information that was rote learnt. In contrast, those who took a deep approach to learning '...started with the intention of understanding the meaning of the article, [they] questioned the author's arguments, and related them both to previous knowledge and to personal experience, and tried to determine the extent to which the author's conclusions seemed to be justified by the evidence presented.'

In later work by Biggs in Australia and at Lancaster University, inventories were developed to standardize the questions asked of students about their study (eg Biggs, 1993). The sequence of questions was shown to be a reliable means of more easily finding how students view their study and intend to approach a task. In the course of this work another approach to learning was identified – the strategic approach. This may differ qualitatively from deep and surface approaches. While these two approaches are more closely identi-fied with reference to the quality of the learning, the strategic approach concerns the way a learner chooses to tackle a task.

In taking a strategic approach, the learner seeks to gain from a learning or assessment task, for example, in terms of grades or in self-esteem or the esteem of others. If she knows she will only achieve what she wants through a deep approach, she will use it. If a surface approach to the learning is adequate, she will use that approach. Those who adopt strategic approaches learn to become alert to the cues that guide them in the nature of learning that is demanded by the task or its consequences. They will tend to find out as much as possible about the demands of any assessment tasks or the preferences of any instructors who are relevant to their success in learning. Since they are not necessarily interested learners, they might not be the ideal students of traditional higher education. However, a strategic approach to learning is likely to be prized in workplace situations where the ability to be efficient and effective in learning – particularly in cost-benefit terms – is desirable.

The strategic approach might also be said to be the ideal approach for the required learning on a short course so long as what the learner perceives to be the target for her learning is appropriate. A situation in which the difference might arise is where the target of the course is the improvement of some procedure in the workplace, but where the component skills and knowledge, that have been the subject matter of the course, are tested at the end of the course. The strategic learner may do well in the test at the end of the course, but not in then applying the learning within the context of the workplace. It depends where her perceived rewards lie.

The distinctions between deep, surface and strategic approaches to learning are somewhat stereotyped above and elsewhere in order to display the distinction between the approaches. This has become evident recently in the application of these ideas to Asian students in academic education. Kember (1996), for example, indicates that memorization can be a strategy in a deep approach to learning where the intention of the learner is to understand the meaning of the material.

There are some references to emotional concomitants of deep and surface approaches to learning. A group of students was interviewed during the revision period for their examinations. Those who adopted a deep approach implied that their learning gave them a sense of satisfaction. Sometimes it was an 'aha' response as 'confusion on a particular topic was replaced by insight' (Entwistle and Entwistle, 1997). Sometimes it was a sense of being now able to understand something that had previously not been clear. There was a sense of 'provisional wholeness' in their learning, a sense that something was 'clicking into place or locking into a pattern', though there was a potential for more learning at a later stage (Entwistle and Entwistle, 1997).

The Entwistles found that the students adopting a deep approach were able to talk about their learning with a sense of confidence that they could explain it and apply it elsewhere. The idea that there is a level of learning that must have taken place in order that the subject can explain her learning in a coherent and sensible manner is important for the later development of these ideas about learning and the process of instructing (Chapters 5 and 6).

In contrast to the deep approach group in the same study, surface learners did not feel confident enough to explain their learning and, in emotional terms, they were apt to feel panicky and anxious about the prospect of the forthcoming assessment. Their surface approach did not give them sufficient coherence in the material in order to represent it in an explanation or application. They might have thought that they 'knew' it, but either their sense of 'knowing' itself, or their judgement as to the kind of 'knowing' required, was defective. They probably did 'know' isolated bits of information, but not in a manner that they could relate them to whole ideas, or apply them.

Learners are not consistently deep or surface learners. A strategic approach, by definition, involves using different strategies according to the task. Most learners appear, however, to have a tendency towards one approach or the other, which is based, presumably, on a tendency to view learning tasks in a particular way.

The descriptions of surface and deep approaches to learning accord well with Berman-Brown's description of the distinction between knowing and understanding above. In Schuck's descriptions of the kinds of learning that she observed in computer operators in the workplace, initial learning was characteristically a surface approach, showing incoherence and little attempt to make meaning. In the later stages of their learning, there was perception of a relationship between the physical action on the computer keyboard and the deliberations about its consequences in the context of an anticipated outcome.

There are links between the layout of the SOLO taxonomy (described above) and deep and surface approaches to learning. In other words, there is a link between the approach to learning and the quality of the representation of learning. The implications of this are crucial. An example of research that illustrates that link between approach to learning and the outcome of learning is that of Van Rossum and Schenk (1984). They set a task for first-year psychology students. The students were asked to read a piece of text and answer questions on it. Before they did the reading, they were asked about the approach that they anticipated using for the learning and about the kinds of questions that they anticipated being asked. The students' actual responses were allocated to the various levels of the SOLO taxonomy by trained judges. The quality of the responses correlated well with the approaches that the learners had taken to the reading task. Learners who had adopted a surface approach could not represent their work at more than a multistructural level. This is hardly surprising. We have earlier suggested that the use of a surface approach to learning implies that there is little attention paid to the ways in which the meanings in the material is integrated either in itself, or in relation to the knowledge and understanding already possessed by the subject. Those learners who adopted a deep approach to their learning were able to represent their learning according to the higher levels of SOLO, but it was noted that other factors could limit their success. On the basis of the manner in which this limitation acted, Moon (1999) suggested that the approach to learning might determine the 'best possible representation' of the learning, while other factors could act as limiting factors to the actual outcome (see later).

Meaning and the process of learning

In this section we begin to move towards a model of learning which aims to incorporate observations about learning that have been described in the sections of this and the previous chapter. It is a model that brings together promising elements from a range of theories that describe aspects of learning. We start from metaphor. We have made reference to a number of metaphors for learning and many of these imply that learning is built up bit by bit in a cumulative manner. A metaphor to describe this idea of learning is the building of a wall of bricks of knowledge, perhaps with knowledge found to be incorrect, simply being replaced. Previous knowledge represents a foundation on which more knowledge is built but no more than that. Such a model accommodates the idea that teaching is like 'bricks' of knowledge to the learner – a common view of learning and instruction.

However, such a model as this does not really allow for a distinction between knowledge and understanding or deep and surface learning. Nor does it allow us productively to explore why a learner does not learn what is taught, or how constructivist views of learning can operate, and it does not imply that previous knowledge plays any more in the process than the provision of a base or foundation for later learning. It is also a passive view of learning with the learner only a receiver.

In the introductory chapter, in the introduction to constructivist approaches to learning, we described Kelly's conception of man as an inquirer, an active agent involved continually in trying to make sense of the world that he perceives. In this view, learning is an active process of seeking to make meaning. New meaning is constructed both from the perceptions of the new material of learning and the relevant prior knowledge and understanding. This view emphasizes the active role of a learner in the adoption of a deep approach to learning, but returns to the notion of building bricks for surface learning which might be called an accumulation of knowledge approach.

In the constructivist view of learning, a more useful metaphor than the brick wall is a vast but flexible network of ideas and feelings with groups of closely linked ideas/feelings. In the network some groups are far apart and some near to each other and there are some relatively isolated ideas that have no direct links to the network. On this model, what is already known or understood and is already part of the network, plays an important role in guiding the seeking and making meaningful of new material of learning. This is the process of assimilation in learning (Piaget, 1971). Unlike the brick wall metaphor, the material of learning does not just accumulate as knowledge but the new material of learning itself can influence change in what is already known or understood. This is the process of accommodation (Piaget, 1971). On this basis, with reference to the deep – surface learning continuum, we could either say – the deeper the learning, the more or more profoundly the network will accommodate to a new state, in response to the new material of learning. Or, we could say – the more profound the change in the network the deeper is the learning.

The term 'cognitive structure' has been used to describe the network of accumulating knowledge and understanding and associ-ated feeling or emotion – 'what is known' by the learner (Ausubel and Robinson, 1969). In the view of learning that has been described above, there is an important development beyond this – that the cognitive structure is not simply an accumulation of knowledge/ understandings and feelings, but it acts as a guide for new learning. In other words, what we both choose to pay attention to, what we choose to learn and the meanings that we make of the learning, are modified by our previous knowledge/understanding and feeling. There is a consequence of this for the interpretation of meaningfulness.

If the cognitive structure is conceived in the manner described above, then that something is meaningful is a judgement made by the learner by relating the new material of learning to her current cognitive structure. A judgement of 'meaningfulness' cannot technically be made in the abstract or by another person. This brings the discussion back to the stance taken by Kelly.

A good illustration of this point is provided inadvertently by Ausubel and Robinson (1969). These (American) writers try to argue that the three letters 'lud' will not be perceived by a learner as meaningful because the learner will not have associations for it in her cognitive structure. On that basis, they suggest that meaningfulness is a quality of the material of learning and that the cognitive structure is simply an accumulation of knowledge. In fact, anyone aware of British comedy is likely to have meaningful associations, for 'lud' in the colloquial response to a judge ('me lud'). This makes the case that something is meaningful because it can be related to existing knowledge in the cognitive structure and that 'meaningfulness' is a quality of the learner's cognitive structure in relation to the new material of learning (Moon, 1999).

The nature of meaningfulness in the constructivist approach is crucial for the relationships between the processes of learning and instruction. If meaningfulness were to be a judgement that could be made directly of the material of learning, this implies a much closer relationship between the material of instruction and the material of learning. The instructor would know what is going to be meaningful to the learner. However, if, as we are suggesting, meaningfulness is a judgement only to be made by the learner, then the automatic relationship between instruction and learning is absent. If, as it appears, 'learners can create any number of meanings, intended or otherwise, out of the same learning experience' (Winitzky and Kauchak, 1997), judging what is meaningful to a learner becomes basically a matter of informed guesswork because the instructor does not have access to the brain of the learner. However, the accuracy of the guesswork can be enormously increased through experience and careful consideration of the cues provided by the learner as to her state of understanding of the material of learning. Angelo and Cross (1990) suggest the devising of simple and frequent tests that provide feedback about the state of the learner's understanding for the instructor. Here, however, we are straying from the matter of learning to that of instruction (Chapters 6 and 7).

The degree to which accommodation of the learner's existing cognitive structure occurs in the process of learning something new will vary. It is directly controlled by the learner's effort to balance the relationship between the new material of learning and the existing cognitive structure. However, external factors, including the instructor, will influence this process. A highly motivated learner on a short course that is of great interest to her, knowing that the new material of learning is going to change the way she operates in the workplace, is likely to allow considerable accommodation in her cognitive structure. Another learner, who does not really want to be on the course, may be there because her manager perceives it as useful. She may not be willing to change her work practices – and she is unlikely to be willing to allow her cognitive structure to accommodate. She may directly reject, or not pay attention to, the new ideas, or will use other areas of cognitive structure to justify the rejection of the course by developing new arguments against its content.

The content of most material of learning that we encounter is relatively as we expect it to be. In this context, 'expecting' something means that it is relatively in accordance with our cognitive structure as it is at that time and the processes of assimilation and accommodation are minimal. Sometimes, possibly because the learner is in a particular emotional or cognitive state, new material of learning provides a considerable challenge. An example is where new material of learning challenges personal beliefs or self-concepts that have become embedded in a personal orientation to the world. Accommodation in such a situation represents a large number of changes in attitude and behaviour, the demands may be too great, and defence mechanisms may operate in force to defend the *status quo*. If extensive accommodation initially occurs with regard to the immediate subject matter, it may take some time for other areas of cognitive structure to become consistent. For example, a change in political belief may imply the adoption of different attitudes to poverty – and the development of different understandings of why people are poor. It might mean going out to a different place for local party meetings, and so on. Short courses can be situations in which these kinds of profound shifts occur but changes may continue to occur for a long time afterwards.

A map of learning and the representation of learning

There are links and correspondences between elements of the learning process – for example between coherence of response – as shown by the SOLO taxonomy and the approach to learning. This, and other correspondences, suggests a model or map that draws these ideas together. Such an attempt is made in my earlier book (Moon, 1999). The word 'map' was used because the exercise was an attempt to unify a range of ideas into a 'whole' that could be more useful than the sum of its parts. 'Map' also gives the sense of a process of plotting and building – not a finished entity that might otherwise be called a 'model'. The map is of learning and the representation of learning since it takes account of the fact that we can only demonstrate our learning through representation. However, it also suggests that we learn through representation of learning (see later).

A version of the map of learning and the representation of learning is presented in Figure 3.1. It is based on the important finding, that the relative depth of learning has a direct affect on the capacity of the learner to represent the learning (Van Rossum and Schenk, 1984).

The map includes the notion of cognitive structure, as described above. The cognitive structure is conceived as what the learner knows/understands already and it has a guidance function for new learning. New material of learning is assimilated into it and it may accommodate its structure in response to the new learning. Degree of depth is presented on the map as a notional continuum between deep and surface learning described in five stages from just noticing something to deep learning which is meaningful for the learner. The surface stages are represented by 'noticing' and 'making sense'. The progressively deeper stages are 'making meaning', 'working with meaning' and 'transformative learning'. In the text above we introduced the term 'best possible representation of learning' (BPR) as a means of suggesting that it is the relative depth of learning that acts as the main limiting factor to the quality of the representation of

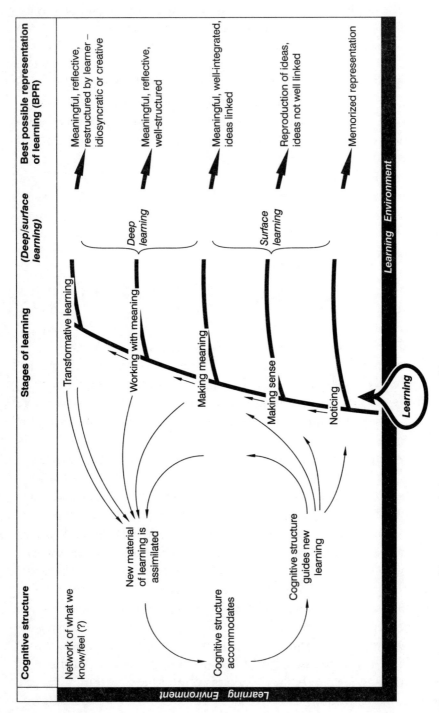

Figure 3.1 *A map of learning and the representation of learning*

the learning. The stages of learning are described and illustrated in the text below in relation to the 'best possible representation'.

'Learning environment' is an element on the map and has been discussed in Chapter 2. It can influence the learner's learning process in many ways, but, in line with Kelly's views (Kelly, 1955) and those of the constructivists, the relevant 'environment' is that which is perceived by the learner. A factor in an environment judged by one learner as a block to her learning might be seen by another as encouraging her learning.

Stages of learning

The description of the map of learning and the representation of learning are based on the stages of learning that are presented in the map. The text is based closely on that in Moon (1999, pp 141–46) and some of the text is quoted directly.

Noticing

'Noticing' broadly accords with perception – when the sensory data is derived from the material of learning. It is a first 'gatekeeping' stage when the cognitive structure guides and organizes the input of the material of learning on the basis of expectations and previous experiences, frames of reference and other personal styles of noticing. Other factors are important such as what the learner knows already, the perceived and given purpose for the learning. A learner looking through a book or papers for material that is of value in writing a report quickly rejects a large volume of the material by relating what is on the page to the purpose of the search and what she already knows. Emotional reactions to the material of learning may be such as to encourage or discourage continuation of the learning. Similarly, the quality of attention that a learner is paying to the material of learning will be a variable at this stage as well as in deeper stages of learning. Noticing something is the prelude to deeper learning. One responsibility of an instructor is to draw the attention of learners to what they should/need to or might be interested to learn.

Moon illustrates the quality of learning though a series of comments that learners might make if this is the extent of their learning:

- 'I might need to come back to this.'
- 'I've just noticed the bit of information that I need.'
- 'I'm anxious. I can't do more than memorize these notes so near the exam.'

If representation of learning can occur directly from the stage of noticing, it will be a memorized representation that is modified from the original mainly by inaccuracies of perception and loss of the point of recall. It is very much in the realm of surface learning. The 'best possible representation', at this stage, differs from the original material in what is forgotten, or what is inaccurate because it was perceived wrongly or distorted in memory.

Making sense

'Making sense' is seen as a process of becoming aware of coherency in the material of learning and organizing and ordering it, slotting ideas together on the basis of relatively superficial similarity. It might be the form of processing involved in elementary problem-solving where there is no advantage in using substantial previous knowledge. Again, it is a surface approach to learning. The kinds of comments that might reflect this stage of learning are:

- 'Does this make sense to you?'
- 'Let's get the gist of this for the exam. I can do no more.'
- 'Does this chemical compound belong in this group or the other?'
- 'I think that we have enough facts to sort out this problem now.'

The best possible representation at this stage might have some coherence in itself but will not be connected to deeper or broader meanings and it will not have involved anything more than superficial integration. In terms of the SOLO taxonomy, the representation will be at multistructural level or lower. On the map, it is described as 'Reproduction of ideas, ideas not well linked'.

Making meaning

In the earlier stages of learning, it seems reasonable to suggest that learning is largely a process of assimilation and that not much accommodation occurs. In other words, the ideas are not deeply linked into existing understandings. At the stage of 'making meaning', it is envisaged that there is some accommodation – some concern with meaning and understanding rather than just 'knowing. 'Making meaning' is the first of the three stages that represent deep learning on the map – learning that seeks meaning and understanding and that relates new learning to current knowledge and understanding in the cognitive structure. In terms of academic learning, 'making meaning' could be seen as the form of learning that is the basis of the productive accumulation and deepening of learning over a period of time. This might be associated with the building of understanding of a subject or discipline. Illustrative comments about this stage of learning might be:

- 'How do these ideas match those that we considered last week?'
- 'What you have just said really fits in with my ideas.'
- 'I understand the reasoning behind what you have just said.'
- 'I am trying to get my head around this now.'

Ideas are now linked together and there is some evidence of a holistic view of the learning. In the terms of the SOLO taxonomy, the representation of the learning will show the qualities of the relational structure. It is described on the map as 'Meaningful, well-integrated, ideas linked'.

Working with meaning

The latter two stages of learning as represented on the map are somewhat different to the first three in that they may take place out of contact with the original material of learning. Indeed, the original material of learning may have been assimilated into the cognitive structure, which may have accommodated, so the original material is now modified as part of the cognitive structure with the potential to guide more learning. The learner may dip into external resources for more information as her actions are guided by the ongoing interactions between the new material of learning and the cognitive structure. Where the representation of the learning is required, there is a manipulation of the meaningful knowledge towards a specified end – the sense of clarifying thoughts on a particular issue. Some other commonly experienced cognitive activities that might appear to involve this kind of processing are:

- organizing thought about something;
- the processing that supports planning something substantial;
- summarizing;
- thinking over matters following an event in order to sum up or reach a conclusion;
- critical analysis;
- deduction and problem-solving that involves understanding the elements that are involved and how they interrelate;
- thoughtful reasoning;
- marshalling facts as evidence in an argument;
- making a judgement.

In the process of working with meaning, the learner may simply review what she knows without substantially changing understanding. She might, in this way, become more aware of what has been tacit – such as the process of becoming aware of how personal knowledge guides her actions in professional practice. Issues in the process of learning at the making meaning stage are illustrated in the following:

- 'Putting these ideas together, I think that I can work out how to present this argument.'
- 'I will need to analyse what this is really saying in order to criticize it fairly.'
- 'Let me sort out my thoughts on this matter and then I will give you an answer.'
- 'Taking everything into account, I suggest this as my next move.'

The representation associated with 'working with meaning' is likely to have the qualities associated with extended abstract structure. It is likely to be a meaningful account that involves other personal or previous knowledge in a manner that suggests reflection and a holistic view of the learning. This enables the learner to be capable of using her learning to give good explanations. On the map, the best possible representation is described as 'Meaningful, reflective, well-structured'.

Transformative learning

There are references in the literature to what appears to be a more sophisticated stage of learning than 'working with meaning' (Habermas, 1971). Transformative learning suggests a more comprehensive accommodation of the cognitive structure and an ability in the learner to step outside her own and others' processes of reasoning in order to evaluate the frames of references that she or they are using. This awareness of personal processes of learning and processing information (metacognition) demands greater control over the workings of the cognitive structure and greater clarity in the processes of learning, and representing that learning, than does the previous stage.

A learner at this stage will be self-motivated and will draw the material needed for progression of her reasoning from sources that she judges to be useful. This may occur in processes of discussion and debate. Learning in the transformative stage might be characterized by the following kinds of comments:

- 'I can see that my view was biased in the past. Now I am considering the situation again.'
- 'On the basis of the arguments put forward in the tutorial, I could see it from a different angle. I understand why you think that way now.'
- 'I have rethought all that I said to you the other day. I am concerned that I had been influenced that day by a previous discussion.'
- 'In those days I studied detail but now I defend my position on the basis of principles.'

Representation of transformative learning will demonstrate the learner's ability to take a critical overview of knowledge and of her own knowledge and function relation to it. On the map, it is described as 'Meaningful, reflective, restructured by learner'.

Other patterns of learning

Tentative though it is, the map of learning and the representation of learning promotes consideration of a number of issues. One is the possibility of upgrading learning. We suggest that two processes that enhance learning might occur – the upgrading of learning and learning from the process of representing learning.

The possibility of upgrading learning

In the surface stages of learning – 'noticing' and 'making sense' and the initial deep stage, it is assumed that the material of learning is in front of the learner as she is learning and that no learning can occur without this contact (other than rehearsal to improve retention in memory). In more advanced stages of learning where learning is suggested to result in substantial accommodation of the cognitive structure, learning might take place in a number of stages. Initially it might occur in a situation of instruction, but later, more learning might occur in a situation where the learner is reflecting what has been learnt and linking it to previous knowledge and understanding. This might be a discussion with colleagues in which the context of the recent knowledge or understandings is widened. In this way, learning might be 'deepened'.

An example to illustrate the deepening of learning on a short course is the learner's attendance at a presentation by an instructor. The depth of learning that can occur directly from listening to a speaker is an interesting issue. The learner is not in control of the rate of flow of ideas. Presentations are sometimes not clear in meaning or in the sequencing of the meaning. Questions and discussion might either help or disrupt the flow, the speaker might speak quickly, and at the same time as listening, the learner might be writing notes. Learners, at the time, may be doing no more than 'making sense' of the material of teaching in order to learn it. However, at a later stage, perhaps in syndicate groups or in discussion, or simply in reading over the notes, more meaning can be made of the learning, advancing it to 'making meaning' or deeper learning as the learning is established, reflected on and linked with other knowledge and understanding.

We are suggesting that the accommodation or greater accommodation of the cognitive structure can occur at this later stage, not necessarily in the presence of the initial material of learning. If such upgrading happens then there are important implications for the process of instruction or facilitating learning. It is interesting to note that what is deemed as good practice in instructing appears to be based on an assumption that upgrading or deepening of learning occurs. Effective instructors do not just instruct, they provide means by which the learners can deepen their learning in discussion, by asking questions and by further reading or research on a topic.

If upgrading of learning occurs from the surface stages of learning, it seems likely that it could occur at deeper stages. For example, in 'toying with ideas' and, perhaps, in consulting ideas from new sources, the learner deepens her learning from (for example), 'making meaning' to 'working with meaning' or to 'transformative learning'. Such a principle might lie behind tutorial systems of learning and discussion-based learning.

Learning from the representation of learning

Another practice of good instruction is to make deep learning more likely by asking learners to practise or represent their learning. Eisner (1991) discussed the manner in which more learning occurs when learning is represented – and how, by requiring different forms of representation of learning, a better quality of learning could be achieved. Thus, for example, in traditional forms of education, it would be quite usual to ask a learner to write about a topic in an essay or report. Normally, the learning will be taken to have happened at the initial stage and the representation (writing) might be seen in the context of assessment. The role of representation in learning tends not to be recognized and therefore is not exploited.

Eisner suggests that the learning that results from different forms of representation of learning varies. For example, the learning that results from a writing exercise will differ from that where the learner is required to depict in a diagram or act out an idea. It is not necessarily better but just different and it seems reasonable to hypothesize that it enhances the quality of the learning overall. On reasoning about the nature and functioning of the cognitive structure, we might suggest that the learning from different forms of representations of learning exploits different areas of the cognitive structure and with the different areas, a wider range of networks of meaning may be engaged.

Implications of the map of learning and the representation of learning

Reflection

On the basis of the map of learning and the representation of learning, reflection occurs in the deeper forms of learning, where learning is upgraded, or where learning occurs from the process of representation (which involves secondary accommodation). It does not occur greatly in surface learning. In the processes of learning in a short course, engaging reflection can be particularly important as a means of relating new material of learning to personal knowledge in order that the learning can be used in workplace practice. This is explored more fully in later chapters.

In most of the references to reflection in this book, the time frame of reflective processes is seen as retrospective but there are some suggestions that reflection is involved in planning and anticipation and can therefore have a future time frame (eg Van Manen, 1991). The position in this book is that reflection is retrospective – dealing with what is already known. Perhaps, where we appear to be reflecting on probabilities, or planning, the process of anticipation might involve reflection on knowledge gained from past experience acting in combination with the imagination of the expected event (Moon, 1999).

Another look at experiential learning

There have been a number of references to the cycle of experiential learning, partly because it is so widely described as an important theory of learning. We return briefly to reconsider the relationship of the theory of experiential learning to the map of learning and the representation of learning. If the experiential learning cycle is so widely cited, it must be saying something important about learning that should be reflected on the map of learning and the representation of learning. One explanation might seem to reside in the focus on an 'active experimentation' phase. 'Active experimentation' implies a form of representation of learning that goes beyond simply reproducing the material of original learning – in terms of the map it implies at least the stage of 'working with meaning'. In other words, in order to be able to represent learning at the stage of 'working with meaning', the learner is drawn through the stages of surface learning and, virtually by definition, is involved in taking a deep rather than surface approach to learning.

It is worth considering the level of demand of the learner's learning imposed by different types of representation of learning. For example, if learning is a matter of answering relatively easy (for the learner) questions, the demand on the learning might not be great and a relatively superficial approach to learning might suffice. When the representation of learning is required in the form of a coherent essay – a deeper form of learning will be necessary to support the representation. An oral presentation may require yet deeper learning. Teaching the material of learning meaningfully to another, however, may require even deeper stages of learning. This latter statement supports the notion that one does not really learn something 'properly' until one teaches it. In terms of courses, it suggests the importance of enabling learners to reach the depth of learning in order that they are able to explain something to another.

4

Learning from short courses: the differences between learners

Introduction

The control of learning rests with the learner. If a learner does not want to learn, she will not learn or she will learn something different, such as how to avoid learning. Many factors determine whether a process of learning is successful or not and the factors interact and may be continuous with other factors in the learning environment, including the process of instruction. The factors within the normally functioning learner will either determine the approach to learning that is adopted by the learner or her ability to cope with more or less complex material of learning.

The next two sections in this chapter generally deal with the learner's approach to a short course. The first section deals with factors that are generally subsumed under the notion of 'orientation to the course'. Orientation concerns the learner's rationale for undertaking the course, which is related to what she wants to achieve from it. The section draws, in particular, from a piece of work on students' orientations to higher education studies and from work on differences in orientation to work at different stages of professional development. The second of these two sections concerns the readiness and 'preparedness' for learning on the course. These terms cover a range of factors that link closely with the learner's orientation. However, while orientation concerns the manner in which the learner orientates herself psychologically towards her perceptions of the course, readiness and preparedness concern the learner's skills, experiences and abilities.

The next section concerns aspects of learning behaviour such as abilities, strategies, and learning style. These are factors that tend to affect either, or both, the level of complexity of material that the learner is able to tackle and/or the approach that she adopts to the learning task. Another aspect of learning behaviour in a short course is the learner's ability to think. The section entitled 'The quality of thought' takes a brief look at three studies of the quality of thinking, all of which suggest that there are stages in the development of thought and the understanding of knowledge.

The learner's orientation to a short course

On the basis of a constructivist approach to learning, we cannot be truly objective about the factors that are involved in building expectations of a course (other than by asking each individual). Trigwell and Prosser (1999) talk of the learner living in an 'experienced world' and with reference to their concern for students on a university course, they say that 'the learning and teaching issue is not that of how ...teachers have designed and constructed their subjects and courses, but rather how their students perceive and understand the way they have designed and structured them' (p 59). Many of these factors are emotional or concern the attitudes of the learner to the learning or to the instruction that she anticipates (Boud, Keogh and Walker, 1985).

An overarching element in the learner's orientation to the course is her purpose for learning. Perhaps it is one of the main characteristics of adult learning that the issue of purpose becomes important. Pedagogy, on the whole, assumes purpose as preparation for adulthood or work and in fact, its purpose is often subsumed in the notion of a relevant adult 'knowing best'. For adults, particularly in the context of short courses, purpose is a more complex issue. One source of information about purpose for the learner is the course aims. This should, but may not, coincide with the manner in which any marketing description is designed. Another type of purpose might be that of the employer who perceives a 'training need' and wants to fulfil it through the course. These purposes may be the explicit reasons for engaging on a course – but may cloud the most influential purpose, which will be the purpose of the learner herself. The learner's purpose may be directly related to other stated purposes or it may differ.

In 1997, Beaty, Gibbs and Morgan reported on a piece of research that has implications for participants on courses of any kind, though the work itself was carried out in higher education. The research considered the 'orientation to learning' of students at a conventional university and the Open University. Orientation to learning was defined in terms of 'the complex nature of a student's aims, attitudes and purposes for study' (p 86). It was seen to be a 'useful construct for understanding a student's personal context for study'. The types of orientation described for the students were vocational, academic, personal and social, though it was possible for the same student to have orientations in more than one area. In the first three orientations, both intrinsic and extrinsic interests were described, where intrinsic interests related to personal development in particular. As they are described, all of the orientations could be applied to those participating in short courses (Table 4.1)

The study indicated that the students' orientation to learning affected their patterns of learning behaviour and, consequently, their experiences of learning. A generalization from the research is that we should not assume that learners choose to engage in a course for only one reason – that of success in the course. There may also be other orientations that are relevant to short courses. For example, an 'avoidance' orientation – taking the chance to avoid the workplace for a day or two.

Examples of factors that will influence the development of orientation to short courses are personal situations, prior experiences of the anticipated subject matter, anticipations of the instructor, the location, of learning in general, of the fellow participants. It is the perception of the participant, not apparent realities, that will determine her orientation – so that one learner's perceptions of the credibility of an instructor may differ from those of another and their responses are likely to differ correspondingly.

Table 4.1 *Learning orientations (adapted from Beaty, Gibbs and Morgan, 1997)*

Orientation	Interest, Aim and Concern
vocational	
intrinsic	course regarded as training – concern is career progression
extrinsic	wants qualification – concern is the recognition of the worth of qualification
academic	
intrinsic	intellectually interested – concern is to be stimulated by the instruction
extrinsic	interested in educational progression – concern is to do well
personal	
intrinsic	interested in broadening and self-improvement activity – concern is the challenge of the material
extrinsic	wants to prove capability – concern is feedback on the course and 'passing' it
social extrinsic	wants a good time socially and the concern is for the facilities that support that 'good time'

The interacting effect of factors complicates the picture. For example, the environment of the course might matter a great deal more to a participant who has a social orientation to the course than a participant who has come with the intention of learning significant professional techniques to improve her working practices. Once the participant is engaged in the course, the orientation becomes influenced by the actual experiences of the course and correspondingly the approach to learning that might have been adopted, may change. The material of learning may, for example, be more interesting or less relevant than expected. However, the initial approach to learning, determined by the learner's orientation to the course, may itself dissuade the learner from changing her approach. A surface approach to learning does not tend to generate motivation and a learner who has chosen this approach may have difficulty in engaging in the course at a deeper level. If it also becomes clear to the learner that a surface approach is not sufficient, anxiety can be generated and anxiety, in itself, tends to perpetuate a surface learning approach so that a vicious circle is set up.

Many short courses are in the context of professional development. Gregorc (1973) suggests that a person's stage of professional development influences her general orientation to her profession – her motivation towards personal improvement and her view of her practice. It is not unlikely that there will be participants who are at different stages in their career or professional development on a short course, even if they are doing the same job. Gregorc studied professional development in teachers, but it seems likely that the idea of age-independent progression in professional growth could be applied to other professionals. He says:

> We seem to assume that a teacher, after he is certified, will display 'professional' behaviour... The lack of research and support for a concept of developmental stages in adults is evident in the training and preparation of the professional educator. Irrespective of individual backgrounds, needs and attitudes, each potential teacher is exposed to common courses... Education college faculty and accrediting agencies seem to believe that this preparation results in a miniature 'complete teacher' who merely needs experience to flower.
>
> (Gregorc, 1973)

From observations of the behaviour of teachers and from a questioning of what 'meanings, understandings, and attitudes' lay beneath the behaviour observed, Gregorc and his team identified four stages in professional development. The four stages are described as 'becoming', 'growing', 'maturing' and a 'fully functioning professional'. They analysed needs and orientations at each stage. In terms of educational needs, early on there is a need 'for "a bag of tricks" to handle all situations', later there are 'signs of self-study' developing towards confidence to improvise and cope with unexpected situations and 'self-directed education'.

Gregorc observed that the movement from 'maturing' to 'fully functioning professional' normally does not occur without intervention of another: 'who causes a growing professional to articulate his concepts and analyse his behaviour. [He]...may help him weigh the new experiences, and restructure new concepts while being present to observe, interpret and inform the maturing professional of his behaviour changes...' (Gregorc, 1973). Again, the description of the change touches on the process of making tacit personal knowledge explicit, in order that new ideas can be integrated into practice. Such a process of change may be initiated by short courses, but the suggestion is that a mentor is needed to support the changes as they go on occurring. In other words, in this form of personal and professional learning, a short course may set off a change for which the individual was ready, which has an impact that is much more far-reaching that has been anticipated. Such an effect is probably not unusual.

Readiness and 'preparedness' for learning

Readiness for learning is a concept that has tended to reside more in pedagogy, but there are good reasons for utilizing it in the context of short courses. Readiness to learn concerns the learner's ability to cope with learning of a particular type or at a particular stage. 'Preparedness' is a term that is added in order to expand the notion of readiness into the area of the emotional state of the learner. Both readiness and preparedness are closely related to orientation. On a short course, there is no time to provide much support for learners who are not 'ready' or not prepared to learn at that level or in the manner of the presentation. Below, we highlight a few areas of learning on a short course where these concepts seem to be of value.

A factor that can interfere with learning is the learner's ability to learn independently in relation to course demands for independent learning. The ability to manage one's own learning and become self-directing is learnt over time and those who have only experienced relatively 'spoon-fed' situations may find the demands difficult to cope with (McKay and Kember, 1997). Discussion or brainstorming, for example, might frequently be used in a course to facilitate learning. Those who expect formal inputs in tidy presentations or lectures, may have difficulties in progressing their learning in such sessions where there is a requirement to relate one's own experiences to those suggested by others. Similar to this is the requirement to reflect on prior experiences and learn from them (see Chapter 2). A dependent learner may find difficulties in recognizing her own subject matter as valuable material of learning (Usher, 1985). It is interesting to note that some of the folklore about adult learning suggests that adults are autonomous learners by nature and have a desire to learn from their prior experiences. This is not the experience reported by Usher in the context of an adult course. There was a sense that learning from personal experience was not developing 'real knowledge' and 'real knowledge' is that in texts. When Usher's group of learners did begin to explore their experience, their work tended to become anecdotal, not producing material amenable for useful learning. He comments:

> A teaching situation designed to facilitate learning from experience became one where [learners] not only failed to take responsibility for their own learning but ultimately rejected the process of learning from experience as trivial and irrelevant. The attempt to operationalize the use of experience in a practical way resulted in experience being seen as anecdotal, from which nothing productive could emerge.
>
> (Usher, 1985 p 63)

Usher is describing the lack of a particular study skill that would have enabled the learners to engage in the required learning. A step beyond the processing of experience into a form amenable to learning is the use of cognitive skills that act as tools in the deeper stages of learning. These tools include analysis, synthesis, criticism and evaluation. It is probably the case that a child can operate these skills if the material of learning is at her level of comprehension. While not all short courses will demand great skills in these areas, Schuck's work on knowing and understanding suggests that there can be a deep dimension to learning even apparently simple keyboard operations. The important point here is that the ability to utilize these sophisticated skills on more complex material of learning can present a substantial learning challenge if the process is unfamiliar. Sometimes supportive practice and coaching will enable success but opportunities for this may not be present on a short course and, where there is no assessment of learning, it can be easier for a learner to hide difficulties. As we have suggested above, those who are more aware of their learning processes (metacognitive) are probably at an advantage. They may be more able to articulate and ameliorate the difficulties that they encounter – but they are likely to be the better learners anyway.

Often on a short course, there will be a wide mixture of participants, perhaps some with postgraduate learning experiences alongside others without a degree. Differences and any likely consequences need to be recognized in the planning and management of a short course. However, a positive way of working with the situation is to make an assumption that learning in a mixed group provides an ideal situation for development of these skills through peer influence. The challenge for the instructor is to set up situations in which those who are able learners can demonstrate their skills, and that those who are less skilled can emulate them and practice in a safe, non-judgemental and non-threatening environment.

It is worth remembering also that the manner in which we use the skills to represent learning is culturally determined – and that disciplines and professional groups have their own learning 'cultures'. Thus, engineers on a short course in business management may be relatively 'unready' for the style of learning and representation of learning that is required. It is also worth remembering that instructors may not cross cultures or disciplines themselves, while the learners with whom they work are expected to cope with the change without much preparation for it.

We talked of preparedness for a course as an emotional state. Perhaps one of the ways in which learners might be least prepared for a short course is when they have been told to attend because a gap in their functioning in the workplace has been construed as a deficit that requires remedial attention. For an instructor, the 'closed-down' look of a group of unwilling attendees at the beginning of a short course can present a serious challenge to her ability to instruct, her ability to develop rapport and, as well, a challenge to her self-esteem. It may be important for her to be clear that she is the 'messenger' and not the 'message' and to start from as near to where the learners are in emotional terms as possible in order to encourage greater acceptance of the instruction.

To summarize this section and to demonstrate the potential breadth of it beyond the specific points made here, we draw from a paper that considers the readiness to learn of students who are entering a social work course (Waldman, Glover and King, 1999). While the relevance is to a longer programme of learning, this summary contains some useful interpretations of 'readiness' (within which they include 'preparedness'). The writers suggest that 'readiness to learn' as a concept seems to encompass a mixture of ingredients that require mixing in the correct balance. They include the following in their list of factors involved in readiness to learn:

- Mental preparation – self-esteem and awareness. They suggest that learners need strength in order to cope with the uncertainties. Some short courses confront learners with potential major personal or professional changes.
- Attitudinal issues – 'being open to practising the learning styles required, by initially being informed and aware of those different learning styles'.
- Anticipating the contexts for learning and learning appropriate skills. In the case of this paper, the skills are those of learning from experience which may be relevant in many continuing professional development courses. They describe this as 'developing 180 degree vision in learning situations'.
- Practical preparation. With reference to improving the impact of short courses, this can be wide-ranging in its implications. For example, for the new learning to be implemented on return from the course there may need to be practical arrangements that involve others such as managers, and others involved in support for the change or the change itself. Another form of practical preparation may focus on time management since a major reason for ineffective outcomes of short courses is the lack of newly created periods of time for implementation. Such time is likely to be in addition to that required in managing the workload that may have built up while the participant was away.

As with the orientation to learning discussed on p 82, the effect of readiness may be expressed through the approach that the learner adopts to the learning. We have implied several times that the approach of the learner to learning significantly depends on how the learner views the learning task. Readiness and preparedness for learning seems to be a particularly useful concept in application to learning situations where there is not the opportunity to support learners who are 'unready' or unprepared in a specific area of learning. The concept focuses attention onto induction processes in a course and the ways in which this may be made more effective for learners in relation to the learning and the ultimate impact of the learning. Some aspects of induction are general – expressed, for example, in good precourse information about the content as well, perhaps, as any specific instruction style that might be used, but there are also ways in which preparation focuses on the learning that will be part of the course. For example, in the use of prework (see p 144) and advance organizers (see p 145).

Learning behaviour

This section considers a number of different factors that may either be relatively stable or more labile aspects of learning behaviour. Again these factors are likely to influence learning either through the approach to learning that is adopted, or through the learner's ability to tackle more complex aspects of the learning.

Much is written about various cognitive abilities and styles and their relationship to learning. Some of the ideas are based on research but many are less firmly founded. Among the best-known work on learning styles is that of Kolb (1984) and the later developments of Kolb's work (Honey and Mumford, 1986). Kolb's original work was based on the experiential learning cycle and suggested that people are more and less able at functioning in the different areas of the cycle. An individual's styles of learning are investigated in a questionnaire and presented as a profile of more and less favoured styles against normative data. Honey and Mumford define activist, reflector, theorist and pragmatist learning styles. Although, apparently, these learning styles are developed in early life, it is not clear how stable they might be over time. The method of filling in a self-report questionnaire tends to focus on personal stereotypes, and not always on the real behaviour. It is also not clear how the context of a task might affect the style adopted. Some people seem more able than others to use different styles for different tasks (Harrison, 1991). It is interesting to note the comment of Brockbank and McGill (1998) that the work on learning styles leaves learning as mysterious as ever (p 33).

The role of something that is summed up in the term 'intellectual ability' cannot be ignored in the study of individual differences in learning or working with ideas. Clearly some learners find learning tasks easier than others, grasping concepts more rapidly – but that might again depend on the manner in which the task is presented. The notion of multiple intelligences counteracts the generalizations implied by the allocation of a single intelligence quotient. Gardner (1983) suggested that we do not have just one intellectual ability but many. These include linguistic, logical–mathematical, visual-spatial intelligences, which are seen as distinct from learning styles. The literature of multiple intelligence seems largely to focus on the implications for instruction, and the importance of taking into account these differences between learners.

Another group of factors that relate to the process of a learner's learning are grouped under the term 'strategies for learning'. Strategies may relate to the manner in which a learner chooses to tackle one specific task – but the implication is that some are more stable than this. Pask (1976) identified learners as 'holists' or 'serialists' according to the manner in which they approached a learning task. Holists have a concern for the whole task from the start of their work, whereas serialists approach the task in a more fragmented manner, shifting from one part of it to another without relating the parts to the whole. The ideas behind the holist strategy enhance our understanding of the suggested functioning of the cognitive structure when a deep approach has been taken to learning. A holist strategy takes account of the context of the whole learning task in guiding the learning of specific elements of it. In contrast, the serialist adds one element of learning to another without initially having a means of structuring the whole.

Moon (1976) studied strategies in reading for learning in a piece of work that clearly supported that of Pask. Readers were given a section of text to read in order to answer questions on it afterwards.

There were two extreme forms of the strategies adopted. In one, the readers read the text from beginning to end in a serialist manner. In the other, the readers shifted around in the text, going back and forth checking understandings and the structures of meanings – a holist type of approach that appeared to accord with the general description of a deep approach to learning. Particularly significant in the research were the interaction between the strategy used and the verbal (linguistic) intelligence of the learners. Those who succeeded best in the test on the text were either those who were high on verbal intelligence (in which case reading strategy did not appear to matter), or those who used the 'back and forth' strategy regardless of their level of verbal intelligence. This research seems to suggest that strategies, abilities and styles of learning interact and that the learner can learn to compensate for a lower or less effective perform-ance in one area by greater use of another. It is again interesting to return to the finding that learners who are good learners in their disciplines tend to be metacognitive – they are aware of and able to utilize effectively their skills of learning (Ertmer and Newby, 1996). This sort of finding, of course, does not indicate whether they are able because they are metacognitive, or whether metacognition accompanies their general ability.

There are many other examples of individual differences in learn-ing. Hartley (1998) mentions some that he calls 'fundamental', such as age, sex, culture and anxiety, and a number of learning styles in addition to those above (eg convergence and divergence in thinking and those functioning better in verbal versus visual modes and vice versa). He provides examples of preferences such as better functioning in morning or evening and preferred seating positions.

An overview of the literature on styles, strategies, habits and capacities in learning (to be summarized as learning abilities and preferences), suggests that there must be some overlapping in the characteristics of the learning process that have been identified. Secondly, it would seem that there is no one ideal way of learning effectively or that would have become obvious in all the research that has been conducted. These observations suggest that skill as a learner can be derived from metacognitive awareness and a variable combination of general intellectual ability and well-used strategies, which may compensate for one another.

It is unclear how different kinds of learning task induce the learner to shift between the abilities and preferences, and the degree of flexibility that is usual. Similarly, it is unclear how much different styles of instruction might favour different combinations of learning abilities. The finding that good learners seem to be more aware of their learning abilities seems to corroborate a notion of the learner being in charge of a range of abilities, which can be deployed differently in different conditions to greater or lesser advantages.

Arising from the observations of learner behaviour, there are a number of issues for the process of instruction. These are summarized below:

- Should instruction be geared towards the apparently preferred learning style, pattern of abilities or strategy of a learner, or should learners be 'stretched' to cope with any style? This dilemma rests on two different approaches to learners – whether they are to be valued only for their learning of the material of instruction at the time, or whether their ability to learn is valued alongside their ability to deal with the curriculum material in question. While the latter position is favoured in continuing professional development and lifelong learning agendas, the general ability to learn might not be the concern of a trainer who sees learning on short courses to be a means of fulfilling a training need.

- We have suggested that instructors may tend to instruct on the basis of their perception of learning. Their perception of learning is likely to be influenced by their personal abilities and strategies. If their practices of instruction emanate from the narrowed frame of reference of their own patterns they might not help learners with different profiles.

- Generally it seems reasonable to suggest that the instructor who is more aware of the variations in patterns of learning and instruction, and of the range of influences on learning, can be more effective in facilitating learning.

The quality of thought in short course learning

We have suggested that learning strategies, styles and abilities discussed above, as theoretical concepts, seem to overlap in practice, and as qualities of learning, appear to interact and compensate for each other. We now add another quality of learning. The work on stages of thinking has implications for learning and for our conceptions of knowledge and understanding.

This section is based mainly on the work of three research groups who used different terminologies but generally who focused on the process of thinking and the understanding of the structure of knowledge. Since thinking has relevance to all areas of learning, these studies might act as a framework for the incorporation of many other variables in the learning process.

The three studies along with others imply that the conceptual basis of human thinking passes through qualitatively different stages. However, these studies differ from many others in being concerned with functioning into adulthood. While in the earlier stages the quality of thinking can have a relationship to chronological age and/ or maturation, the relationship is soon lost. For all but a few individuals, the progress through stages stops before they have reached the most sophisticated form of thinking. The point where progress ceases seems largely to be determined by the educational and self-development processes in which the individuals are involved.

The general point to be made in this section is that participants in a specific short course may often be mixed in their ages and in their levels of formal education and life experience. They are therefore likely to be at different stages in thinking, some still progressing and others not developing at present. The situation is probably different from those encountered in formal education where the sophistication of thinking is likely to be less variable on a particular course. The mixture of different levels of thinking in a group can have major implications for instructional processes.

The studies described in brief below, showed that people appear to progress from assumptions that knowledge is certain, towards the understanding of knowledge as a construct and, therefore, uncertain. This has implications for any manner of working with meaning and in particular in problem-solving and decision-making.

The earliest of the three studies was that of Perry (1970). Perry studied American male college students over the period of their studies, looking at intellectual and ethical development through a relatively unstructured interview technique. He found that there appeared to be identifiable stages in the development and he observed that students progressed through the stages at different paces, reaching different levels of sophistication by the time they completed college.

King and Kitchener (1994) also found that their mixed gender group of subjects demonstrated a similarly staged development in their ability to make judgements. In the seven stages that are identified in this extensive experimental work they noted the evolution of thinking from a 'pre-reflective' stage with knowledge viewed as stable and certain. When knowledge is perceived to be absolute in this way, there is no room for the greater development of that knowledge through reflective thinking. In the highest two stages only did the researchers note 'true' reflective judgement in which the learner recognizes uncertainty and understands that there may be no 'right' answer to a dilemma, only a 'best solution'. At earlier stages, learners could reach solutions to problems through the use of problem-solving techniques, but these were of no value in working with uncertain knowledge.

Belenky, Clinchy, Goldberger and Tarule (1986) confined their study to a group of women of a range of ages. Like the other research groups, they distinguished stages and, although they do not present these as a progression, the suggestion of a hierarchical arrangement is present. Women whose thinking was least sophisticated were said to be receivers of knowledge from others. Those who were most sophisticated realized that the knower is a part of the construction of knowledge – with the implication that knowledge is seen as neither absolute nor objective.

It is not surprising to note that characteristics of the more sophisticated forms of thinking, described in the studies above, have features in common with the more sophisticated forms of learning described earlier in this part of the book. For example, 'transformative learning' implies the capacity of the learner to 'step outside her own and other's processes of reasoning in order to evaluate the frames of reference that she/they are using'. We have suggested that such a learner will…'draw the material for her progression of her reasoning from sources that she judges to be useful'.

It is relevant to this text that King and Kitchener considered that Perry's highest identified stage was lower that those that they identified with their larger and older group of subjects. This may suggest that there may be changes in the sophistication of thinking beyond that demanded by a first degree. However, it is improbable that many short courses would challenge learners at this sophisticated level of thinking. This deficit might represent a neglect in our conceptualization of professional development.

In the same way that learners may be in different stages of readiness or preparedness for a short course, there may be individuals at different stages in their thinking ability. This will not matter if the material of instruction is low level but it may matter if the material of learning is more complex. With little time to provide individual support on a short course, as previously described, it is useful to design instruction in such a way that learners can learn from each other. They need to understand that thinking processes differ and that some more sophisticated material demands more sophisticated thinking and understanding of the nature of knowledge. Kitchener and King indicate that progression through the stages of thinking occurs when learners confront a challenge to their current thinking patterns.

5

Instruction and the facilitation of learning: the context of instruction

Introduction

The next two chapters will focus on the ways in which the instructor influences the learning of participants. However, we start in more general terms – by returning to aspects of the relationship between instruction and learning. As with learners' views of learning, instructors' conceptions of learning, of learners and of teaching, influence their choice of technique. Some different conceptions of instruction are reviewed in the second section.

Relating learning and teaching

Good instruction takes account of learning

In Chapter 2, a distinction was drawn between the activity of learning and the activity implied by the words that describe instruction. The distinction is needed because of the frequent confusion between words describing instruction and learning and in order to make clearly the point that learning can happen independently of instruction. The activities of an instructor, however, cannot logically occur without the presence of a learner, although the learner may be distanced in location and time. Despite this, it is not unusual for the subject matter of discussions on improving learning to focus largely on the teaching process with little reference to learning. It is the contention of this book that the process of learning must be in the forefront of considerations of instruction.

The reason why learners need to be taken into consideration in the manner in which an instructor instructs is clearly articulated by Schuell (1986) in the context of higher education: 'If students are to learn desired outcomes in a reasonably effective manner then the teacher's fundamental task is to get students to engage in learning activities that are likely to result in their achieving those outcomes'. Schuell goes on to point out that it is the activities of the learner that are more important in achieving the outcomes than the activity of a teacher. The link between instruction and learning will be expanded in many different ways in the next chapter.

Constructivism, instruction and learning

At the core of the view of learning that is presented in this book is the idea that the learner constructs meaning and herself controls the nature of material of learning that makes up her learning activity. Constructivism applies at the level of the learning content as well as to the learner's perception of the learning situation. We have suggested, for example, that learners, whose orientation is towards achievement, will tend to adapt their learning of content to what they think is required of them in a given situation. In situations of formal instruction with assessment, this means that they will tend to want explicit guidance from the instructor about the assessment task. This means, in turn, that the instructor will need to understand how her manner of communication about learning and the learning outcomes for the programme are perceived by, and how they are likely to affect the learning of, learners.

However, as well as the learner constructing her view of learning, the instructor will also make sense in her own way of learning in general, of the needs of the learners with whom she works, of her teaching task and the demands of the programme. As with the learners, her perceptions of instruction and learning will arise from her prior experiences of teaching and learning, her conceptions of learners, of the expectations on her from others – and so on. The next section explores conceptions of instruction.

The conceptions of instruction

Organizational dimensions

Many factors contribute to a conception of instruction. For example, an instructor often works in the context of an organization (Reid, Barrington and Kenney, 1992). Organizations have general orientations to training or instruction. The process may be confined largely to high-status staff (elitism); staff may be seen as able to decide for themselves their training needs (voluntarism); or training is seen as a facility that staff may use to further their own development (humanism). In contrast, training or instruction decisions may be imposed (authoritarianism). Beyond these intra-organizational orientations to training there are national initiatives influencing attitudes towards vocational training, such as national vocational qualifications, that provide another influence on the instructor's conceptions, of her activity. In recent years the term 'continuous professional development' (CPD) has come to the fore. This incorporates the notion of lifelong learning – or the need for staff to be flexible in their approach to education and work, 'updating' their learning as necessary (Reid, Barrington and Kenney, 1992).

Beyond these general orientations, Reid and her colleagues consider some attitudes towards the role of instruction and training within the organization and the relationship between the trainee and the organization. The provision of a learning opportunity might be seen as putting an obligation on the learner to the provider. It also raises issues concerning the decision as to who decides that the learner needs instruction and what its content should be

Similar influences can affect other educational organizations. It is important to note, however, that the existence of an espoused approach to education does not mean that the approach is always translated into the processes within the institution or organization. For example, McLean and Blackwell (1997) observe that the higher education institutional view of teaching tends to propound the significance of critical thinking and questioning, whereas much actual teaching is 'tidy' (p 54) and encourages students to learn the content of lectures, handouts or set textbooks. The acceptability of learners going 'beyond the given' seems to vary according to the discipline. One reason for this divergence is the increasing number of students which, in turn, complicates the methods of engendering the traditional outcomes of higher education.

Conceptions of instruction and the process of learning

The institutional or organizational orientation to learning may or may not be transmitted through the instructor. Fox (1983) provides a useful starting point for consideration of conceptions of teaching – which similarly illustrate different attitudes to the processes of the learner. The setting for his work was a polytechnic and it is probably significant that those he studied were in the early part of their careers and their views of teaching might well have been inspired by school experiences – and hence they are likely to be applicable to other sectors.

The first group of 'theories' that are identified by Fox are the 'shaping theories'. In these, teachers see themselves as 'shaping' or 'developing' students towards some kind of 'end' that might be a learning goal or a profession. Sometimes these theories take on a more 'electrical' form, being then concerned with the activity of appropriate 'wiring up' of learners.

Fox described another group of theories as 'transfer theories' in which the material of teaching and the material of learning appear to be seen as coinciding, since teaching is a process of transferring material of teaching directly to the learner. The learner is relatively passive and Fox points out that clichés such as 'imparting knowledge' have the same basis. These two theories relate to the ideas that learning is like building a brick wall of blocks of knowledge. The instructor dispenses the bricks in an appropriate sequence.

Fox suggests that the 'travelling theory' puts the instructor in a role as a guide, or leader, showing the way to learners who might be seen as travelling on a 'learning journey'. He describes this as a 'developed theory' because the learner is now a participant rather than a passive receptor. Another developed theory is the 'growing' theory. Here the student's mind is to be nurtured by provision of an appropriate environment. Growth is not determined by the teacher, but by the grower. Fox distinguishes between these two latter views of teaching – suggesting that, while both are concerned with the student and her learning, travelling theory takes more account of the subject matter of the curriculum.

An instructor's orientation to instruction and learners is evident at many levels. Forsyth, for example indicates a transfer view of instruction within the context of a variety of approaches (Forsyth, 1992). For example, he reminds the reader that 'understanding' is always 'diluted' in the process of training (p 63) and that there should be a concern with 'how much of the message…[is] being taken in' (p 64). As befits the transmitter of a message, there is concern with the image of the trainer regarding her clothing, whether she stands rather than sits, and in ensuring that she is seen as 'important' (p 65). An instructor who is more learner-centred in approach might actually choose to sit and reduce her importance in order to avoid dominating communication that occurs between participants.

We have commented already on descriptions of training in a flow diagram or in sets of arrowed boxes. This can suggest the notion of a transfer process of instruction rather than one that recognizes and responds to the detail of the learning involved. Reid, Barrington and Kennedy (1992) comment that 'the definition of a relatively simple set of procedures in a simple sequential model…is unlikely to describe best practice…'. For example, 'evaluation' is usually placed in a discrete box of its own when, in good practice, it must occur all of the time – as part of every boxed activity.

Not only are there differences in views of instruction within and across educational cultures, but there are also differences in what instructors aspire to do and what they feel they actually do. In a recent discussion on a mailbase discussion list (ISL@mailbase.ac.uk, January 2000), a variety of metaphors for instruction were shared. They included juggling, being a manager of multiple needs, musical conductors, lighters of fires, fillers of containers and so on. Many of these metaphors appeared to describe 'the way it is' for teachers rather than the way it could or should be.

These ways in which instructors view their role in the process of instruction, in the context of this book, are of little significance if their style does not influence the manner in which learners learn. Perhaps, at this point, we should acknowledge that a sufficiently resourceful and self-directed learner will learn what she wants or needs to learn regardless of the influence of an instructor. We talk, therefore, about the majority of learners who await that influence, with their mixtures of orientations to learning, styles and strategies, and views of teaching and learning.

Prosser, Trigwell and Taylor (1994) not only considered the conceptions of teaching among a group of (24) higher education teachers, but also the effects of their conceptions on learners. The following conceptions of teaching were held:

- teaching as transmitting concepts of the syllabus;
- teaching as transmitting the teachers' knowledge;
- teaching as helping students to acquire concepts of the syllabus;
- teaching as helping students to acquire teachers' knowledge;
- teaching as helping students to develop conceptions – ie the learners build on previous learning;
- teaching as helping students to change conceptions – ie the learners are willing to change ideas that were formed in the context of previous learning.

These conceptions of teaching broadly match those identified by Fox. Some are teaching- and curriculum-centred and some are more concerned with the learning process of the learner. As with Fox, this list would seem to have wider application than just in higher education, although a conception that is perhaps not represented here is the extreme of the teaching-centred view in which the quality of presentation is paramount. This is reflected in Forsyth's orientation, mentioned above, though it is clearly evident in the comments of some higher education teachers in Trigwell and Prosser's studies.

The important issue for this book, however, is the relationship between conceptions of learning in the instructor and the effects that it has on student learning. Trigwell and Prosser describe a series of studies that have demonstrated that in their work on university teachers, those teachers 'who focus on their students and their students' learning tend to have students who focus on meaning and understanding in their studies. University teachers who focus on themselves, and what they are doing in instruction activities, tend to have students who focus on reproduction.' (Trigwell and Prosser,

1999, p 142) In this way, Trigwell and Prosser relate the quality of teaching to deep ('meaning orientated') and surface ('reproduction') learning. Biggs (1999) usefully coins the terms 'deep' and 'surface' teaching.

Below, we expand on what is implied by 'deep' and 'surface'. However, it is important to consider what we are saying in making these research-supported statements about instruction and learning. Clearly, in terms of short courses or any other learning, we are valuing the qualities of learning that are associated with deep approaches and therefore, largely, we are valuing learner-focused instruction that encourages learners to take a deep approach.

'There are no right ways to teach'

In real life, things may not be quite as simple and learner-centred teaching may take unexpected guises. The association of learner-centred teaching with deep approaches to learning appears to be straightforward, but there may be issues that arise in other learning situations than higher education that complicate the picture. Learners in higher education are there by their own volition and most have some concern to achieve academically within the context of their own orientations (Chapter 4). In schools, however, children are not present of their own volition and may reject the learning, the teachers and the schools. Beyond cajoling through reward and sanction there is little a teacher in this situation can do to engender a deep approach to learning since learning is not contingent on teaching. When a class is large, with some wanting to learn and some rejecting everything, a reasonable approach is to focus on the quality of presentation that at least has the chance of gaining the attention of the more motivated learners. It is not unusual, in the context of short courses, for some learners to be similarly disengaged, and sometimes consciously or unconsciously to be as disruptive of the process of instruction as can school children. In such situations, focus on the quality of presentation can be a valuable – and, in a sense, a learner-centred strategy.

We have said there are many factors beyond instruction to which learners may variably respond in the situation of a short course. They may change their orientation to learning during a course. An individual on a course meeting a highly attractive member of the opposite sex might change from an orientation that favoured a deep approach to learning, to a social orientation in which surface learning predominates. Similarly, a feature of many short courses is a sumptuous lunch and this can considerably alter the receptivity of learners in the early afternoon. Instruction patterns that successfully worked before lunch can fail utterly after lunch. Working with learners requires continuous awareness and modification of approach to instruction.

We have recognized that learners have a range of learning styles and strategies, which they can deploy in various ways, including compensation. The effective instructor has to take account of the differences in learners through deployment of a range of styles and strategies of instruction that relates to the learning, compensating with one for another as necessary, and as her skill will allow. This seems particularly important for short courses where there is little opportunity for 'catching up' if things fall behind for reasons of ineffectiveness. There may simply not be time, for example, to let the learning process lapse into a soporific doze after lunch. Basically, the relationship between learning and teaching is unpredictable (Harvey and Knight, 1996), and for effective results relies on continual adjustment on the part of the instructor and the learners both to themselves and to their environment.

Learner-centredness means that the instructor is aware of and responsive to the state of learning. It does not represent a position that instruction is based solely on the initiatives of learners and that information-giving is unacceptable. Such a process of instructing/ learning can be inefficient and tedious for all involved. It is not the kind of instruction implied by the notion of learner-centred instruction in this book. The need for awareness and responsiveness of the instructor to the learners is emphasized even more strongly in short courses where time and efficiency are of major importance.

The next chapter explores the implications for action of learner-centred instruction and we sum up this section with a fitting introduction to the next: 'There are no right ways to teach, only better ways' (Marton and Ramsden, 1988).

6

Instruction and the facilitation of learning: the facilitation of learning for impact

Introduction

The previous chapter has indicated that, as is the same for the concept of learning, there are different conceptions of instruction and these can influence the learning of learners. An approach to instruction that enables learners to change their conceptions of the subject matter with which they are working is the means of encouraging good-quality learning. Where the learning is to have impact on the work practice, there is greater justification for engendering a deep approach to learning among participants. The main part of this chapter concerns the activities in instruction that engender a deep approach to learning. However, we have indicated that good instruction is more than facilitating deep learning in individuals. The next section considers the activities of an instructor to orchestrate the learning of a whole group towards successful learning. The last section is concerned with more general techniques of instruction.

Facilitation of learning for impact

Learning that is to enable the participant to do something differently in the workplace requires a number of qualities. At a simple level, it requires coherence. The component ideas in the learning need to interrelate and represent a 'whole'. On the SOLO taxonomy they need to be at least relational and such that learners understand the point of the learning and can apply it to a familiar situation (Biggs, 1999). The map of learning and the representation of learning in Chapter 3 demonstrate how that the attainment of these qualities of learning implies the necessity of a deep approach.

It is worth considering the challenge for the learner of applying new ideas in the average workplace. In many situations it is easier simply to carry on in the familiar pattern of working and not to institute change. In addition, the application of new ideas can require time, thought, and may stimulate adverse reactions from colleagues and sometimes managers who are concerned to maintain the momentum that has already been disrupted by attendance at a course. These are all reasons why the new learning needs to be meaningful, understood and ready to apply, rather than memorized in bits and pieces.

There are several pertinent issues. For example, what are the qualities of the instructor's action that can encourage deep approaches to learning among participants on a short course? There is another question that is relevant to short courses particularly because of the time factor. The instructor is not just working with one learner – she is working with a group of learners and her task is to facilitate effective learning in the whole group. What does she need to do to bring the learning of a whole group to the appropriate outcome? Most of the literature that explores ways in which the approach to learning is related to instructional processes does not seem to take into account the difficulty of facilitating meaningful learning in a whole group. We have shown that within any group of participants, there will be many differences (Chapter 4). The role of the instructor is not, then, just to change conceptions of learning, but to orchestrate a mass of changes of conceptions in learning towards meaningful approaches in as many participants as possible. She will need also to take into account those who will choose not to change their conceptions – perhaps because their orientations to learning are social or are for 'a day away from work'.

There are, therefore, two issues here. The first matter is the identification of the qualities of instruction that facilitate meaningful learning and the second involves the management of the diversity of participants so that the best possible impact may be achieved in the whole group. There is much overlap between the two.

We reiterate the first question above: what does an instructor on a short course need to do to engender deep approaches to learning that, in turn, facilitate impact in the workplace? Discussion is organized under the following headings that are worded as strategies to support meaningful learning (with the considerable overlap recognized). The word 'manage' is used with cognizance that it can be misinterpreted. It implies here a process of awareness and monitoring by the instructor so that equilibrium is maintained that best facilitates meaningful learning:

- working with a holistic view of the course and its structure;
- managing balances in time and workload;
- managing a positive emotional climate of learning;
- managing the attention of learners;
- managing the depth of learning;
- monitoring the progress of learning.

Working with a holistic view of the course and its structure

It is important that those who instruct on a short course have a view of the whole course. Generally, it is reasonable to expect this of any instructor, even one who has not designed the course – but sometimes several people might be involved or there are guest presenters of specialist elements of a course. It is not uncommon for guest presenters to demonstrate inadequate briefing. When there is a concern for the impact of the learning on practice, a continuous orientation to the whole course is crucial with every element recognizably contributing to the whole.

Chapter 1 indicated how the intended learning outcomes of a programme could be of two types – some of which relate to the learning at the end of the taught part of the course, and some of which relate to the practice in the workplace. These two types should be clearly related so that the learning in outcome statements for the end of the course is the same as that applied in the workplace.

The knowledge of the structure and progression of the course towards specified outcomes needs not only to be in the instructor's mind as she instructs. It also needs to be in the minds of the participants so that they know how the parts of the whole fit together and how they anticipate the impact of the learning on practice. In a constructivist view of learning it is the sense that the learner makes of descriptions of a course structure that is critical, not the words given. This means that aim and learning outcomes of a course should be openly discussed – not just presented as part of the marketing material – and there needs to be a sense of progression or outcomes – a conscious system of 'signposting' for the learners.

There are a number of ways in which the direction of learning is 'signposted' before the course, and at the beginning of or during a course. Some generalizations are made here, to be discussed in greater detail in Chapter 8 as components of a course. One form of sign-posting is to provide learners with an orientation to the course in the form of 'prework' or advance organizers. A slightly different function again is served by the precourse 'briefing discussion' suggested by Harrison. She suggests that such a discussion will 'establish with the learner exactly what the purpose and objective of the event are, and how they relate to the learner's needs; also how learning will be used in the work situation once the learner has finished' (Harrison, 1991, p 248).

Effective summarizing is also a form of signposting since it locates progress-to-this-point within the context of progress towards the whole. This may involve the learner's summarizing activity rather than that of the instructor, since it is what learners understand to be a summary that matters, as long as it bears some relationship to the learning outcomes. There are also events that may occur at the end of a programme that serve to ensure that the learners have a coherent view of the content of the programme and how their learning is intended to relate to the outcome statements. Such a debriefing would ideally occur twice, firstly with reference to the course learning and later when the learning has been put into practice.

Another major element of 'signposting' activity in learning and the facilitation of learning is the 'flow' of content. Chapter 7 suggests a framework for the content of a course that, in turn, promotes the impact of learning on practice. Flow is also shown in the subject matter in the sequence of detailed, general principles and the evolving expertise in processing ideas. It is interesting – and perhaps initially surprising – to observe that the specifics or details of subject matter often precede the development of generalities. In schools, children engage in working with examples of laws of physics and chemistry before they are led to observe the generality of the laws themselves. Similarly, Marton and Ramsden make a case for the development of general expertise in learning to be expected to occur in the context of more specific learning: 'We should teach specific knowledge domains in such a way that the [learner's] general capacity is developed at the same time' (Marton and Ramsden, 1988, p 274). Poor structuring or the lack of a holistic view of a course can occur, in particular when:

- a course is 'pre-packaged', and simply taken on by an instructor who uncritically transmits the content as indicated in instructions;
- when parts of a course are 'lifted' from elsewhere on the basis that they provide 'roughly' the right material;
- when 'guest presenters' are drafted in to instruct elements of a course without sufficient prior briefing;
- when an instructor is simply not 'on top' of her material, its sequence and overall structure. She may not have run the course for some time and has not reviewed it before the event. She moves from one element to another, perhaps legitimately in response to questions from participants, but without being able to retain or return to an overall picture.

It is interesting to note that the metaphor of instruction that underpins these situations is usually one of transfer (Chapter 5) – either from instructor to learner – or from initial course developer to current instructor to learner. A good instructor will have a sense of ownership of the material of teaching and a deep sense of how it fits together and judgement as to the most sensible sequence for presentation of it for this group of learners.

Managing balances in time and workload

It is uncommon to talk of time in respect of instruction and training and yet the timing of instruction has a substantial link to the quality of learning that occurs in a session or over the span of a course (Sheal 1989, Biggs, 1999). There are at least five aspects of time that are worthy of consideration, though there is a considerable overlap between them:

- sufficiency of time in which to reach the intended outcomes;
- workload for learners in relation to time;
- the pacing of learning and instruction;
- intellectual space;
- 'wait time'.

Because a short course is short and usually finite, there is a tendency to try to squash in too much instruction or content or both. When it becomes evident that planning has not allowed sufficient time in which to reach the learning outcomes, there is also a tendency to cover material in haste. A characteristic of hurried instruction is that the focus moves from the learner to the process of instruction – the concern is to 'cover' material rather than to ensure that learning occurs. Haste in instruction militates against meaningful learning.

Haste in learning also militates against meaningful learning and it is usually manifested in a high workload. There is plenty of research that suggests that learners tend to adopt a surface approach to learning when they feel 'overloaded' (Entwistle and Entwistle, 1997). When anxiety about learning also provokes a surface approach to learning, some unfortunate vicious circles can be generated. The allocation of high workloads for learners in a course can be a deliberate policy on the part of course organizers in order to minimize the time taken out of normal work.

The pacing of instruction draws in the matters discussed above, but also concerns the design of a programme. Pacing concerns the sequencing of intensive work with work at a slower pace that might involve some summarizing or reflection (see below). The considerations of pacing might concern learner attention (see below) or the optimizing of learning so that practice or summary sessions are placed appropriately in relationship to the initial presentation.

The last two aspects of timing probably deserve much greater attention in the literature. Presumably because of the predominance of metaphorical 'theories' of learning that emphasize transfer and therefore raise the role of instruction in the enhancement of learning, there is a tendency to 'over-teach'. The result is that there is little time for learners to process the material of learning and process it in relation to their meaningful understanding of it. We have introduced Barnett's term 'intellectual space' to describe the need for learners simply to have time to think about what they have learnt. Intellectual space may not be as necessary for those taking a surface approach since there is probably less processing of the learnt material. Chapter 8 gives a consideration of the means by which meaningful learning can be encouraged through the use of periods for reflection built into a course.

'Wait time' may differ from intellectual space only in duration. It is a term used to describe pauses in the speech of instructors. Tobin (1987) describes experimental work that shows that learners benefit from these pauses during instruction. The pauses give them time to process their learning. Pauses might be made naturally or deliberately, though wait time is probably part of the practice of good instruction. There are useful techniques that provide wait time, such as asking a rhetorical question. Part of the technique of providing wait time is the development of tolerance of moments of silence during a presentation.

Managing a positive emotional climate of learning

The emotional environment of learning includes the expectations of learners, the course ethos and atmosphere, any sense of anxiety or optimism, or enjoyment or flippancy. It would be possible to fill the book with details of possible influences on learners – but on a constructivist view of learning such objective descriptions would, in some degree, be pointless because it is the individual's perception of the environment that affects her learning. The deliberate development of a 'relaxing' environment for one individual may seem too 'unworklike' for another. However, there are some general points that are worth making.

The first point concerns the expectations of the learners. We have touched on expectations in terms of the orientation of learners, and the anticipations of the kinds of learning that would be expected in the course, and we have discussed the manner in which these factors influence the approach to learning taken by the learner. The development of advance anxiety about a course is a particular problem when it encourages the adoption of a surface approach to learning.

Another form of expectation is that described by Thomas (1992). From his research on training, he found that, 'Many people admitted that they attend training events expecting to spend some proportion of the time being bored either by the quality of the presentation or by the fact that what they are being asked to learn or do bears no practical relation to their real needs.' Expectations of a good practice in a short course can be heightened by efficient initial administration, which may include material to work on in advance (prework, p 144).

The setting of a course can considerably influence the emotional orientation of learners to learning but, as with other environmental factors that affect learning, the learner's perception of environment determines many of the effects. However, extreme discomfort or noise are likely to affect most learners. The principle of limiting factors also comes into play and the point at which any disturbance will affect learning might be modified by other factors. For example, great enjoyment of the course could militate against the negative effects, while for a course perceived as boring, even a reasonable environment could be deemed negative.

There are some practitioners who argue that putting substantial efforts into the ambience of a setting is crucial to learning. For example, Lawlor and Handley (1996) suggest that it is necessary to stimulate right-brain activity in a course, both because there will be some 'right-brain dominant' individuals and because stimulation of the right hemisphere makes use of 'untapped potential' (p 5). Since the right hemisphere 'seems to be attracted by colour, art and music' (p 5), they suggest the use of these environmental stimulants in the form of pictures, themes, mobiles, 'welcome notices' listing participants' names, and so on. These ideas are supported by the literature of accelerated learning that holds that the process of committing to memory is enhanced when individuals are relaxed and the alpha state of brain function is invoked. Slow movements of baroque music are said to encourage this state (Rose 1985).

A key word in the discourse of accelerated learning might be 'memorization'. The need to 'memorize' suggests the favouring of a transfer theory of learning and tends to oppose the notion of meaningful or deep approaches to learning. This writer cannot process ideas at a deep level in the presence of music! The notion of limiting factors is relevant in that the environmental factors in learning influence the process only at their extremes – and the tolerance levels at the extremes may be modified by the influence of other factors.

When things 'go wrong' on a short course, a generally negative climate can set in. This may be tinged with cynicism if the credibility of the instructor is questioned. Biggs (1999) makes some helpful suggestions about how to avoid the development of negative or cynical climates. He describes the influences of learning climate on learners – with the positive extreme characterized by a trust by the instructor that the learners will function best given freedom and opportunity to use their judgements. The other end of the scale is represented by negativity, perhaps towards a course and the learners. Cynicism and anxiety are bred in the latter climate. Some examples of this negative behaviour by instructors in short courses are:

- inappropriate controlling behaviour;
- the discounting, without consideration, of opinions that may differ from theirs;
- the ignoring of negative comments from learners;
- a sense of disengagement from the subject matter (eg 'You'll hate this but we've got to cover it', Biggs, 1999, p 64);
- grumbling and blaming others, blaming circumstances, etc.

It is fair to recognize, however, that instructors on short courses are often agents of the provider and are often not responsible for environmental shortcomings. Yet they are the only representative who is visible to the learners. Short courses are often conducted in situations that are not familiar to the instructor, and which she has not chosen. She may not be responsible for the unavailability of the promised handouts, the missing pages, the fact that the overhead projector focusing knob spins without effect, cramped seating, and so on. She then has a narrow path to tread to maintain her credibility with the learners by detachment from blame, and yet must not to be too negative about the circumstances into which she has unavoidably stepped or about the credibility of the course providers.

In Biggs's words, the attitudes of learners, their expectations and the approach to learning that these factors support, 'depend critically on what [learners] are most likely to attribute their failure and success to. How these attributes are built up is partly cultural, partly upbringing and partly what goes on in the classroom.'(Biggs, 1999, p 65) When things go wrong, the role of the instructor may well become that of a juggler (p 100), trying to keep many factors still in play – with the focus on the provision of support for meaningful learning.

Managing the attention of learners

The management of attention in a course again does not seem to be a topic to which reference is widely made and yet for those who design courses it should be a major consideration. On the map of learning and the representation of learning (p 70), the first stage of learning is termed 'noticing'. Paying attention – or noticing – is a prerequisite of learning and when attention fades, learning performance will fade at the same time. To take a deep approach to learning requires more effort and more attention from learners since more mental processing is required.

It is a characteristic of many short courses that one instructor works with a set of learners in one location on the same area of subject matter for a continuous period of time, and in formal education such a situation would be unusual. On this basis, short courses may require that more concern be paid to learner attention and, even in the most interesting courses, attention may wander for a variety of reasons. Some reasons are physiological and are not under the control of the learner, unless she is able to change her level of physical activity or her state of arousal. A learner may have difficulty in making these changes without causing disruption. An instructor needs to be vigilant as to the state of attention of the group, recognizing her power of control over arousal and activity.

There are some predictable aspects of the management of attention of learners on a short course. Attention tends to be high in the beginning of a course and at the beginning of the day. It is likely to wane before lunchtime and it is very likely to be low in the early part of the afternoon. Generally after a day on a course, attention will tend to drift down towards late afternoon. A quality of a good instructor is the possession of the capacity to gain the attention in participants. Some of the methods will have been built into the design of the instruction in advance – probably anticipating the pattern of attention described above. Other methods of gaining attention are to be used as the need arises and some of these come under other headings in this chapter (eg changing pace). Changing the level of physical activity is probably the most effective manner of gaining attention when it is flagging. This does not imply the immediate recourse to physical jerks. A change for learners from listening to writing may be sufficient though something more active may be needed to regain attention in a warm room in the early afternoon. Similarly attention is raised when learners are required to be more responsive such as responding to questions, laughter, involvement in games ('energizers') and simulations, or work in small groups which necessitate interaction. If all else fails, having an unscheduled break is far better for the process of learning and the credibility of the instructor than flogging on when everyone is half-asleep.

A short course is short, however, and with this in mind (and apart from simply having a break) there are good ways and not such good ways of changing attention. Good ways of changing attention are still focused on the goals of impact on practice. Some games and small group work reinforce the learning and the learners may not realize that the pattern of activity has been changed in order to raise the attention level. Activities that are pure games with no relevant learning may be indulgences of time on a very short course.

Managing the depth of learning

Since there is a range of different ideas included in this subsection, bold print is used to distinguish each part. We have suggested that the adoption of a deep approach to learning is an important quality of learning, though will probably only occur if the factors that are described in the subsections above are favourable (eg attention to learning). A deep approach involves the learner in wanting to learn for meaning, wanting to understand the material of instruction and to relate it to her previous understandings while, at the same time, being willing to change these. There are a number of features of instruction that will encourage a deep approach to learning.

Firstly, **a learner will need to know what it is that she is expected to learn and how she will know when she has learnt it**. There are many ways in which such information is conveyed. However, Sotto's words set the issue in a suitably broad context before we narrow it to the classroom situation:

> ...people learn when they discover that they don't know something (which they consider worth knowing), form hunches about a possible answer, seek information, and apply that information to test those hunches. In doing these things they have experiences, and in that way they learn... As for teachers, their job is to help people to discover that they don't know something that is worth knowing; and then to help them to find answers in a reasonably orderly and satisfying way.

> (Sotto, 1994, p 197)

Within the classroom, the aim and learning outcomes of a programme provide shorthand indicators of the learning that the course is designed to address. While this described learning may not entirely relate to the learners' conceptions of what she needs or wants to learn, the statements of intended learning outcome provide a starting point for dialogue or negotiation (Chapter 1).

The role of learning outcomes in providing information means that early on they should be given to learners, and reviewed later. Reviewing learning outcomes is a way of 'signposting' a course, noting what has been achieved and what is yet to be achieved. Sometimes it is possible to say, 'We have covered these learning outcomes, and in the next session/hour/day we will address these.' Sometimes learning outcomes span the whole course, being realized at the end of the taught element or in the application to workplace practice.

As well as understanding what they will be able to do that is better in the practical situation after the course (impact), **the process of learning may be monitored**. Not only does an instructor need to understand how to encourage a deep approach to learning, but also she needs to know how to check that learners are adopting this approach. There are many procedures that will enable useful information to be elicited on the quality of learning, only some of which will be recognized as formal assessment.

Assessment tasks facilitate learning because they require **learners to represent their learning** (map of learning and the representation of learning). Learning is represented when the learner expresses her learning in speech, writing, in graphic form and so on. Some informal examples of methods of representing learning are:

- providing an explanation;
- discussion;
- responding to questions;
- being asked to summarize;
- being asked to write notes on something;
- and so on.

When a learner represents her learning, it is usually towards a purpose – to respond, for example, to a question. Reviewing the material in cognitive structure, in order to respond, may or may not require reorganization or reprocessing of the ideas. Based on discussion earlier, the representation might be of knowledge or understanding. For example, 'What are the causes of heart disease?' may mean a reiteration of unprocessed learning. If, however, the question is about the intricacies of advising a particular vulnerable individual how she might avoid heart disease, there is likelihood that the learner will not have knowledge ready to reiterate. She will need to process several ideas in order to formulate a response.

Representing learning is also a way of learning (Eisner, 1991). In the last example above, it is likely that learning about health promotion in the case of heart disease is deepened through representation. Eisner points out further that the nature or medium of the representation will influence the nature of this secondary learning. When the representation is in formal assessment situations, we should be aware of the manner in which learning is directed by the nature of the representation required.

Asking learners to represent their learning probably amounts to asking them to do anything other than sitting and listening. Doing virtually anything with what they have learnt will mean that they must represent their learning – even when they write notes. There is an onus on the instructor to provide contexts for representation that encourage deep learning.

Carl Rogers talked of the importance of **developing a sense of ownership in learning** (Rogers 1969). Ownership in the context of a short course could have at least two meanings. The first is the sense of being in control of the knowing and understanding so that the learner is able to use it comfortably in representing learning as currently required. The idea of knowing and understanding 'well enough for present purposes' incorporates the idea. The other meaning of 'ownership' is closer to Rogers' meanings – and it concerns the development of personal relevance of learning. We have suggested that some people attend short courses because someone else considers that they need to be there. It may be hard for such individuals to acquire a sense of ownership of the learning. For those who are motivated, there can be a much more subtle process of developing ownership that is part of taking a deep approach to learning. It is a reflective process of relating ideas to one's own situation. The instructor cannot make this process occur, but can produce conditions which support it. The provision of appropriate conditions may be a matter of asking learners to talk about how the new material relates to their own work situations. Alternatively it can be subtle and less directed – such as ensuring that learners have time in which to process ideas, encouragement to reflect (see above) or gentle prompting though questions.

Challenging learners could be the opposite of the subtlety. There are at least two relevant meanings of 'challenging' learners. The first is the opposite of spoon-feeding (McKay and Kember, 1997). Learning is not a 'tidy' process and learners need to be confronted with unstructured situations to overcome, in order to improve their skills of thinking (King and Kitchener, 1994). Setting a challenge of this kind for learners requires a reasonable awareness of what is known already, the conceptions of the present material and their relationship to the learning that is required.

A different form of challenging in instruction is when the challenge is deliberately targeted at particular areas of knowledge or understanding where change is desirable. The methods of challenging might be similar to those mentioned for deepening understanding, but more specifically designed to confront issues. Some examples of methods are:

- through debate;
- by 'playing' with ideas with questions such as 'What if…'; 'Supposing…then what?' 'What would be the consequences of…?';
- through focused short questions that individuals or small groups discuss in a short space of time, presenting the response or a brief account of their thinking in plenary;
- the provision of short focused questions for individual response in a limited time or in limited space (or word count);
- the setting of problems for solution by individuals or small groups, and so on.

Challenging learning will be of direct help to some learners but others will need support in changing their ideas. This may mean that there needs to be time for reflection after these exercises.

Like much of the material in this section, several purposes can be fulfilled by the use of any technique. Not only does challenging promote learning but because the activities tend to be at the leading edge of the learning, they provide a particularly effective means of monitoring the learners' understanding and also their abilities as learners – which leads to the next area for consideration.

We have suggested previously that learners who are **aware of their own learning processes** (metacognitive) tend to be more effective learners. One reason might be that their understanding of their functioning means that they are able to use their self-knowledge to modify their patterns in different circumstances or for different purposes. Another is that they are better able to understand that subject matters differ in their structure and presentation and they are more able to adapt to unfamiliar material (Harvey and Knight, 1996). A third reason is tautological. We have associated the ability to be metacognitive with the deepest stage of learning – the transformative stage (Moon, 1999) and we may be saying no more than that these learners are good at learning because they are good at learning.

A way of stimulating learners to become aware of their own learning processes is to ask them questions that relate to their experiences of learning on or before the course. These questions can bring out the differences between deep and surface approaches to learning and the degree to which learners are and have been strategic in their learning. What might be most important here is that learners learn the language with which they can discuss the qualities of their learning. On a very short course this may take too much time, unless it is directly related to the required outcomes of the course (eg a course on facilitating learning in others).

Monitoring the progress of learning

We have deliberately not used the term 'assessment' in the heading for this section because assessment tends to raise stereotyped associations that are narrow in focus. The range of ideas encompassed under this heading is wider. This section relates the monitoring of progress to good instruction, while the relevant section in Chapter 8 broadens the topic and provides examples.

In the context of a short course, monitoring the progress of learning has two meanings and it is important to be clear about the differences when designing means of monitoring them. The first concerns the progress of the learning towards achievement of the learning outcomes. The second concerns the observation of the quality of the learning itself.

In either case, the monitoring may not imply the employment of new activities. In the case of the monitoring of learning towards outcomes, it might mean that the instructor switches her attention to the processes of learning that underlie the manner in which learners respond to some sort of a prompt, instead of attending to the content of it. She will consider whether their responses indicate an understanding of principles or are a reiteration of what has been given. The prompts that will distinguish between the two qualities of learning will be those that require deep processing and reflective thinking, not those that test memory. They may be the same prompts used to challenge learners (see above).

The monitoring process may be based on activities planned ahead to assess learning within the programme or there may be informal tasks that enable learners to demonstrate their progress during the sessions without, necessarily, being aware of the process. There are many quick activities that provide this information – such as asking learners to summarize the content of the previous session. The situation needs to be managed so that the summaries of those who are considered most at risk of not understanding are heard/read.

This will give an indication of the state of learning in the whole group (eg classroom assessment techniques, Angelo and Cross, 1990).

Monitoring processes allow an instructor to change her approach to the instruction or to the quality of learning that she is trying to engender. They provide her with a means by which she can give feedback to learners on their progress so that they can take responsibility for their own improvement. Feedback can be in the form of information or it can be in the form of encouragement or validation of good progress.

Monitoring might not only apply during the course. If potential problems can be identified before the course, extra support, perhaps in the workplace, can be arranged. Asking the potential course members to do some prework (p 144) can be a means of detecting potential problems. Similarly, because we are concerned with the impact of course learning, it is desirable that monitoring should continue beyond the end of the course.

Orchestrating learning across the whole course

We have suggested above that the literature on improving instruction, particularly in the literature of student learning, tends to assume either that the instructor works with single motivated individuals or with a group without individual differences in which members will progress at the same rate. Some of the skills of an effective instructor working with short courses will be concerned with orchestrating the group of learners to achieve the required levels of learning. We use the word orchestration to imply the process of managing a whole learning group in such a way as to maintain progress towards the learning outcomes and improvement of practice for all. The value of this orchestration is better recognized in the context of training and short courses where evaluation is concerned with the effectiveness of the whole course (though sometimes with the emphasis on administration and instructing rather than the results of the learning!). Chapter 4 suggests that there are many potential individual differences among any group of learners. Some examples are:

- readiness for learning;
- orientation towards the course, attitudes;
- prior learning experiences;
- stage of thinking;
- learning style;
- state of knowledge of the topic;
- conceptualization of learning and instruction and so on.

There are many techniques in a short course that can enable the provision of extra support for those whose learning is such that they may not reach the learning outcomes. The deficit may be in the quality of their learning or in their general work towards learning outcomes. However, there is a ground rule. Learning is an activity of the learner – and instruction can only help if the learner chooses to allow this to occur. The logistics of time, space and the lack of instructor person-power may act as limiting factors in determining the management of the situation. Some arrangements or methods that can help are provided in Chapter 8.

Technical skills of instruction

The function of this brief section is to provide balance. The constructivist stance implies that good-quality instruction is that which is geared into the processes of the learners' learning. On the whole that position stands: that where possible the best instruction is guided by the learners' learning, but we widen the notion of good instruction to recognize that there are qualities that are important in all instruction regardless of how the instruction relates to learners' learning. These qualities might be particularly exemplified in guest lecturers who do not have the opportunity to know or interact with their audience. There are also situations where learners overtly or covertly reject learning but have no choice but to be present. Generic qualities of good instruction are listed below with some comments and some references to other locations in the book or useful references:

- A clear, steady and pleasant **voice** (Martin and Darnley, 1996). The voice is not only a vital element in face-to-face instruction, but it conveys much information about the instructor to the learners – anxiety, uncertainty about the material or confidence and expertise. In hearing her own voice demonstrating certainty or uncertainty about the material of instruction, the instructor provides feedback for herself in a cycle that can restore or reduce confidence. The voice also conveys credibility, Cornish says (in the context of teaching): 'A quiet experienced teacher will not need to strain the voice and quiet firm speaking is more likely to produce a well-ordered class. The sound of confidence is catching and we feel safe in the hands of someone who sounds as though they know what they are doing' (Cornish, 1995, p 63).

- **Credibility** is conveyed by the voice, by posture, by demonstration of knowledge in presentation and in responding to questions, and in other ways. The issue for the learner is to feel confident that the material of teaching is helpful – 'Is it worth my while being here, or am I a fool to be listening to this stuff because I think it is not right?' The latter attitude is not conducive to a deep approach to learning – even if the teacher might be said to be 'deep teaching' (Biggs, 1999).

- Credibility is also engendered when **explanation and presentation is clear**, though Brown (1978) suggests that there might be something more to it than that as explanation is judged by the understanding that it engenders: 'for an explanation to be understood, it must be attended to… the explainer must ensure that [her] explanation appears sufficiently worthwhile and interesting for them to do so. Good explanations are, therefore, clearly structured and interesting…[and] obviously poor or inadequate explanations are confusing or boring' (Brown, 1978, p 10). Clarity is a function of the pace, sequence, organization, presence and manner of the explanation in relationship to learner needs.

- We mentioned '**organization**' as a function of explanation, but it is an important feature of good instruction in its own right. Loss of notes, loss of place in notes or inept handling of equipment such as an overhead projector and slides indicate poor organization, which degrades the credibility of the instructor. Short courses are often located in settings away from a familiar base, and hence the possibility of disorganization is greater – though so is the possibility of learning to be more organized!

- Most of the characteristics of good instruction above are predictable, based on what a learner needs from an instructor in order to learn well. Yet the characteristic often most valued in an instructor, when learners evaluate sessions, is her **enthusiasm for the subject matter**. Enthusiasm in an instructor seems to engender enthusiasm in the learner – perhaps through encouraging greater interest or attention. Conversely, there are instructors who seem to think that they can gain empathy with learners when they talk about their boredom with the subject matter. This attempt seems effectively to spread the boredom to the learners.

We conclude these chapters on instruction and the facilitation of learning with a suggestion and an interesting quotation. The suggestion is for any instructor who wishes to think more deeply about the processes of instruction in general and how she operates in a practical situation. Maintaining a learning journal is a means of becoming more aware of processes in instructing, and it provides a place for reflection on them (Moon, 1999a). Chapter 8 gives some suggestions of the uses of learning journals for learners. The suggestions can be equally applicable to those who instruct. The quotation, simple though it is, and true though it often is, has some important implications for the processes of instruction: 'Trainers are very good at doing what they like to do... We must not forget, however, that the function of training is to meet the needs of those being trained rather than those delivering the training' (Thomas, 1992, p 59).

7

Designing courses for impact

Introduction

This short chapter acts as an introduction to the last major part of this book. So far, the chapters have largely been concerned with the processes that underlie the instruction and learning on a course. This has involved consideration of the aim and anticipated outcomes of a course that could be said to furnish purpose. It has also involved consideration of the nature of learning and how this relates to and determines the nature of instruction. Now we start to look how these underlying factors are organized into the activities of a course that in turn enable a learner/group of participants to move towards changing their practice, in accordance with the purpose of the course.

Two organizing ideas are introduced in this chapter as a means of guiding course development – the framework to improve the impact of short courses and the notion of course components that represent groups of activities, which guide learning towards the anticipated outcome or impact on practice. It starts, however, by looking at the process of and rationale behind the process of course design.

Course design for impact

It is pertinent to reinforce again the idea of impact of a course. Unless a short course has impact on what a learner can and does do after it, there is little point in its existence. The notion of impact therefore needs to be seated firmly behind the designing of a course. Course design represents the planning of a course. It may begin with an analysis of training needs or with an expression of a wish to improve work practice – or a bright idea. The anticipated impact then influences the expression of an aim and anticipated learning outcomes. These should preferably relate fully, or at least in part, to the anticipated change in practice, though they may also refer to the learning on the course alone (Chapter 1).

In the usual sense, beyond aims and learning outcomes, course design will address the pattern of activities in the course along the line of the aim that will enable the learning outcomes to be achieved. However, the effect of making impact of central importance on a course means that other activities can be aligned in course design. It is legitimate to consider how, for example, the course administration furthers the likelihood that a course will have an impact on subsequent work practice. Relevant activity in administration might be briefing meetings before and after the course in the workplace about the new practice (Harrison, 1991). While not technically part of the learning on the course, the meetings are relevant to the wider picture of impact.

Going even further back than this, the manner in which the subject matter of the course is selected may have an impact on the implementation of change. In previous chapters, for example, we have discussed the motivational implications of this. It may determine the orientation of the learners to the course and therefore their learning. If a decision about work practice change is made without reference to the potential learner, the motivation is likely to be less. Schuck's concern to develop an environment of inquiry in the workplace is relevant here (Schuck, 1996).

In addition, what happens after the course needs to be taken into consideration in course design. Willis describes the situation in which learners may find themselves after a course:

> A person returns to the workplace, experiments with the skills and uses a new vocabulary. The work group, faced with strange and new behaviours, starts to feel uncomfortable. Although they didn't like the old behaviours, at least they knew what to expect. This nervousness prompts them to make jokes like 'Look who just got

back from charm school!'. In this way people get taught not to use new knowledge.

(Willis, 1993, p 28)

The anticipation of this sort of situation is as relevant to achieving impact as a result of the course as is any other aspect of the learning in the course, and, therefore, has a legitimate place as part of the design of the course.

In the paragraphs above, there is an implicit suggestion that issues involved in course design need to be broadened to incorporate the planning for improving impact. The breadth of view of course design is reflected in the breadth of consideration of course components. However, the chapters on learning and instruction have indicated that breadth is not the only way to address impact. Depth of learning is relevant too. First, therefore, we introduce an organizing framework for courses. In particular, the framework facilitates the development of appropriate learning.

A framework to improve the impact of learning in short courses

The framework presented in this section represents a coherent set of guidelines for courses that seek to have an impact on practice. The framework is based on work on short courses in health promotion (Moon 1996 and 1999). It identifies four stages of learning for a short course that shift the learner towards the anticipation of the application of the learning in new practice in the workplace. It includes, therefore, the idea of transfer of the learning from the course learning to that needed to change the practice in the workplace. The framework is not presented as a rigid format, but rather as a loose guide for the selection of learning resources and learning activities in the course. The framework is completely flexible, to be used in whatever way seems to be most appropriate in the judgement of those designing the course. However, as will become evident in the latter section of this chapter, it has particular value as a means of structuring reflective activities, for example, as a structure for individual reflective activities that accompany a course.

In a similar way to the above, the framework can provide a direction for the material of instruction presented by the instructors – or a checklist, since it is not essential that the sequence is retained. However, the sequence may be used to provide a sense of progression to the course, building from existing practice to the new practice. Depending on how the framework is used, it may or may not be necessary to incorporate it explicitly or implicitly into the learning outcomes. The framework has a theoretical justification that is described in the later part of this section. It is presented in Figure 7.1:

Phase 1: Develop awareness of the nature of current practice

What is your current work practice with reference to this subject matter or these skills? (For example, how do you currently promote health?)

Phase 2: Clarify the new learning and how it relates to current understanding

What is it that you have learnt here/on this course that can improve your practice? (For example, what have you learnt that is useful to you for the promotion of health?)

Phase 3: Integrate new learning and current practice

How does this new learning relate to what you knew and did before? (For example, what are the general implications of the new knowledge/skills for your practice?)

Phase 4: Anticipate or imagine the nature of improved practice

How will you act in such a way that your practice is improved as a result of the learning? (For example, what will you do that represents improvement in your promotion of and education for health – what will you do differently?)

Figure 7.1 *Framework to improve the impact of learning in short courses (based on Moon, 1996, 1999)*

The framework was developed as result of observation on the practices of the operation of short courses. Apart from this, however, there is also theoretical work that underpins the development of the framework – but in stages and not as a whole.

The work of Schön (1983 and 1987) is particularly significant for the first phase of the framework. Schön discussed the relationship of propositional or espoused theory to practice. Schön starts from the suggestion that there is a crisis in professional activity, particularly in the non-scientific professions such as teaching and social work, where the action is determined by the problems faced at the time. The crisis, he suggests, is due to the misunderstanding of the relationship between theory and practice. There is a tendency to assume that the formal theory of a professional subject area prescribes the form of practice but Schön's thesis is that it is the manner in which professions have developed and their pattern of beliefs that determines the functioning of the practitioners. This takes into account the 'unstructured' nature of many professional circumstances that are simply not in the form that makes easy application of formal theory. The distinction in forms of knowledge in a profession accord broadly with the categorizations of Eraut (1994). Such a view concurs with a constructivist viewpoint.

Schön uses the term 'knowing-in-action' for the kind of knowledge that guides action in a practical situation. Significantly for the framework, such knowledge tends to be tacit and the practitioner is therefore unable to describe what she actually does (Polyani, 1966). There are consequences of this for the educational process – since something that cannot be described verbally is less amenable to being 'taught' in the conventional meaning of that word. To overcome this difficulty, Schön promotes the use of a 'practicum' in which professional activity is explored and, with coaching and discussion, is made more explicit, thence becoming amenable to development.

Schön's work justifies the stage of developing awareness of practice, but common sense says that in order to change, we need to be aware of where we are starting from – and hence we do need to be aware of our current practice. It is this idea that forms the basis of the work of Candy, Harri-Augstein and Thomas (1985, pp 100–01): 'if people are aware of what they are presently doing, and can be encouraged to reflect on it and to consider alternatives, they are in an excellent position to change and to try out new ways of behaving…If people's awareness can be heightened, and they can intentionally examine life events, then they can get more out of each experience.' Later these ideas were developed into a system of 'learning conversations' (Harri-Augstein and Thomas, 1991).

Phase 2 of the framework is separated from Phase 1 in that it deals with the new material of learning. The emphasis of this phase is on sufficiently deepening the learning so that it is possible to use it to guide practice. Chapter 3 provides plenty of justification that a deep process of learning is required for the learning to be applied. It is important, therefore, that the approach adopted by learners is a deep approach.

In Phase 2, also, the learner needs to 'own' the learning. She needs to develop an understanding of how the material is to relate to her own activities – the activities that she is now more aware of from her work in Phase 1. Rogers (1969, p 163) describes the importance of the ownership of learning as learning that 'involves the whole persona of the learning – feelings as well as intellect…the learner knows it is his own learning and can thus hold onto it or relinquish it in the face of a more profound learning, without having to turn to some authority for corroboration of his judgement'.

Phase 3 and 4 provide the basis for the transfer of the learning to the situation within the workplace. It represents a further stage of deepening the learning in Phase 3, and then of anticipating how the learning relates to practice and how both will fit into the context that exists. To some extent, this is a matter of anticipating problems and difficulties, but the anticipation is also related to the widely used techniques of using imagination in therapeutic or self-improvement situations. Here, playing through future situations in the imagination has the effect of smoothing the processes of implementation, and of improving the performance (Gallway, 1975).

A variety of course activities, which includes the input of information, can support the various phases of the framework, but, since much of it is focused on the relationship of awareness and the learning to the life of the individual, reflection is particularly significant in the process. Phase 1 will involve reflection on past and present activities in practice; Phase 2 will focus on the new material of learning. The term 'cognitive housekeeping' applies to Phase 3 – as the process of deepening learning (Moon, 1999). Phase 4 is an anticipation of future activity. Van Manen (1991) suggested that reflective practices can be involved in the anticipation of the future. Even if we see reflection as a process applied to material that has already been learnt it is possible to consider that when reflection is on the future, a combination of processes may operate. This might include reflection on past experience, knowledge (the product of learning and reflection) and the imagination of the event (Moon, 1999, p 97).

Components of courses – an introduction

The idea of course components

Throughout the next chapter, a range of course activities will be introduced under the heading of course components. The ultimate rationale for considering course design in this way is that in order to achieve effective impact in the short time for learning on a short course, every part of a course should contribute to this – even elements of the administrative practices. There is no time to engage in course activities that are there purely because they have become traditional activities. To achieve this shift in thinking and the full orientation towards impact, the notion of course components is introduced.

A course is usually made up of many different activities that tend to have common identities across courses and that are the basic units for the development of a course. Examples are brief presentations ('lecturettes'), group 'rounds', games, small group sessions ('break-out groups'), and so on. Moon found that it is possible to identify a limited number of roles or functions that these activities fulfil (HEA, HEBS, HPW and HPANI, 1995). The same course activity can be employed with different functions depending on the way in which it is used or structured. Thus the use of small groups may deepen learning (Chapter 3) or it may increase the social ease among the whole group so that they learn better from each other (Chapter 2).

These functional areas of work in a course should be purposeful and should contribute to the learning outcomes and, particularly in the context of this book, to the final impact of the course. Sometimes, however, it seems that the units of activity are being used for some intrinsic value – such as pure enjoyment (for instructor and/or participants) or because they just happen to be seen as 'something that is done in groups'. In these cases, their use is not intelligently tied to a purposeful function and the course could be said to be drifting. It does not matter if a longer course 'drifts' for a while but it does matter if a short course drifts as there is so little time. It seems helpful to identify the kinds of functions that support successful learning that will enable the course to have an impact on workplace practice. We use the term 'course components' for these groupings of units of course activity under the functions that they fulfil.

The idea of course components identified by the function that they serve, links the many descriptions of course activities in the popular literature to the purpose in a course that they serve, and to the overall outcomes that the course is meant to achieve. The important point about course components that we are making in this book is that the components and their constituent activities should be related to the intended impact on practice.

In the context of course components, the framework that is described in Figure 7.1 may play one or more of several roles. It can guide the deployment of course components towards the achievement of impact or it may provide a structure to reflective activities that shift the learner towards her anticipation of the impact that her learning will have on practice.

We are not necessarily saying that the course designer will think of design directly in terms of the components (identified below), but that she will think of the function that the course activities serve. This thinking can ensure that – even if an activity is used for regaining the attention of a flagging group – it is, at the same time, facilitating learning in an appropriate direction.

Some components of short courses

In the first consideration of courses in terms of components (HEA, HEBS, HPW and HPANI, 1995), eight course components were identified for short courses in health promotion (then called course activities). After some rethinking in the context of the more general approach of this book, 12 components have been identified, but this is not a fixed number. The idea of courses having components that are identified by their function, like the framework, is intended to be a useful idea that helps in the development of effective courses. It is therefore open to reinterpretation and it is probable that, for specialist courses, there might be new areas of function that are not identified in this account. The activities that make up the components of courses are discussed in the next chapter and include the following:

- course planning or administrative activities;
- activities that involve actual instruction or the delivery of information;
- activities that facilitate group functioning to improve the learning resource of the group;
- activities to support the learner in implementing change in practice;
- provision of overviews of the course – introductory or summarizing activities;
- activities to deepen or enable integration of learning (other than reflective activities);
- reflective activities;
- activities to support individual learning or coping behaviours;
- assessment activities to evaluate personal learning;
- course evaluation activities.

The components above are not mutually exclusive. Some are very close, but because they play a slightly different role in the process of the course or the progress towards the improvement of impact on practice, they are considered as separate. For example, most activities that are reflective will tend to deepen learning, but they are separated because the reflective activities may be used to underpin the sequence of the framework to improve the impact of learning.

The sections on the components in the next chapter do not cover each component exhaustively. There is much literature that describes the activities of short courses, though not with the more purposeful approach of this account. Much of the material does not need to be repeated here, as the relevant books are common on every shelf of a staff development or training library. The following chapter will therefore only describe activities that are unusual or are those that have a particular relevance for working towards the application of the learning in practice.

8

The components of
a short course

Introduction

This chapter is devoted to the description of the components of
short courses that were introduced in the previous chapter. The
sections on the components below do not pretend to cover each
component exhaustively. The descriptions, therefore, concern notes
of guidance or activities that are unusual or that have a particular
relevance for working towards the application of the learning in
practice. As we suggested in the previous chapter, activities play a
role in more than one component because they have different
purposes. The sequence in which the components are listed is for
convenience of description. However, we reiterate the point that
in a short course, each activity should be chosen in relation to the
intended course outcomes and anticipated impact on practice.

Course planning or administrative activities

While many course planning and administrative actions cannot be
counted as contributing towards the impact of a course on practice,
some can be an important influence. These generally fall into three
main groups:

- those in which the participants can be helped to have confidence that the course will enable them to change their practices;
- actions that ensure that the expectations of the participants are matched where they are reasonable;
- planning so that learning time is maximized.

The first two of these points are close. In terms of the development of the participant's **confidence** in the course we have suggested in Chapter 6 that the credibility of the instructor is important to enable the participants to feel that their learning is being effectively managed towards the desired impact on practice. The instructor may either manage the administrative processes or is supported by them and if participants sense efficiency, they can more confidently expect that the identified course outcomes can be reached. Here are some examples of the way in which administrative activities might convey confidence that there can be impact on practice:

- Precourse material is couched in terms of change of practice (where this is possible).
- The expected outcome statements are made explicit early on and are related to the structure of the course that is described – possibly before the course.
- The participants are helped to feel that their workplaces are relevant to the course, eg by a participants list circulated in advance.
- If there is to be assessment it is discussed early and is related to the anticipated effect on practice.
- If there is briefing before the course, again this focuses in terms of an outcome of change in practice.
- Any follow-ups to the course are explicitly concerned with the impact of the course on practice.

The second point about the **reasonable expectations** of the participants may be as concerned with avoiding the development of negative attitudes that can seriously disrupt the progress of a course as about good practice. A series of little things going wrong at the beginning of a short course can seriously damage participants' attitudes to it. For example, handouts printed incorrectly might be forgiven, but combined with a lack of biscuits at mid-morning break and a noisy group in the next room, these factors can amass to disrupt learning.

Other things that often 'go wrong' in a course concern the number of participants (too many and too few for the location), poor instructions or directions over time, a mismatch between what people think the course is to be about, and what it is about. In the last case, briefing may have been poor or insufficient. It may be worth going to some length to meet participants' expectations in order to avoid the negative attitudes developing. Sometimes there are 'no-win' situations, such as when half of the participants are late and half think that the instructor should proceed (when that means stopping regularly to welcome latecomers).

The third area is an activity of **planning**. The length of many courses is not only determined by the ideal time in which to learn the material, but by other factors such as the length of time that can be afforded. Even if the total time available for a course is finite, the arrangement of that time may be flexible. Thus two half-days with a period in between can be more effective for learning if learners are expected to follow a task (and learn more) in the period in between. This is particularly useful if the period in between is in the workplace and preparatory work towards change of practice can be done – perhaps part of the framework activity (Chapter 7).

Another way of extending the period over which a short course is run is by setting prework (see p 144). This is work that is done in advance of the course, which can create a mindset towards the subject matter in advance. It may require that some preparatory work be done in the workplace before the learner attends the course (eg talk to a manager or colleagues about the proposed changes in practice).

Learning on a course may be extended at the end by use of an assessment task that requires learners to continue to think about the material. It would be useful to ask learners to reflect on the manner in which they have implemented the change in practice and solved problems that have arisen. Sometimes it is possible to arrange a meeting after the course where learners make presentations about the changes that they have instigated as a result of the learning – again, the preparation for the presentation extends the period of learning.

Activities that involve actual instruction or the delivery of information

There are many ways in which information may be delivered with plenty of detail about method provided elsewhere. The point made in Chapters 5 and 6 is that there is a lot more to instruction than delivering information if the learning is to be of a sufficient quality to be employed in the improvement of practice. The following are some of the ways in which information can be given and follow-up activities may deepen the quality of the learning as is necessary. It is worth considering the differences that are implied for learning by the different techniques of instruction, and similarly for the course as a learning environment and for the process of learning. For example, there are likely to be fundamental differences in all three aspects between the processes of explaining and of giving a lecture or formal presentation (Brown, 1978):

- lectures, 'lecturettes', presentations, explanations;
- material or notes to read, information sheets;
- material online;
- exercises which carry information, eg simulations;
- various media such as video or audiotape;
- overhead projector slides;
- peer instruction (see p 148).

There are better and less effective means of instruction for promoting learning, many of which are described in Chapters 5 and 6. One distinction that needs to be made in the design of instruction is whether the material is of central importance to the course or whether it is support material. There may be a dilemma, for example, in how much extra material to provide in **handouts**. It is possible that there is no 'right' answer here. Some participants are naturally interested in wider reading about a topic and some will feel over-whelmed and even annoyed at having more than is needed for the topic of the course. Others will feel interested at the time but will never get around to reading the extra material and hence it is wasted. Among some learners, there is a tendency to use handout material as a 'prop' and where none is prepared, there is a request for copies of any overhead slides. In terms of promoting learning, sets of printed overheads are rarely a substitute for a well-introduced and prepared handout or well-listened-to presentations. We may dissuade participants from writing notes, but to write notes is to purposively interact with the material of teaching, while to ask passively for copies of overheads can mean that little effort is put into learning.

Apart from clarity and structure and other more obvious qualities of presenting material, the **pacing** of instruction is probably more important than is usually recognized. Pacing can refer either to the very short-term pauses, or longer gaps. Wait time and intellectual space were mentioned in Chapter 6. Longer-term pacing introduces short periods for reflection or linking new ideas to practice. This is discussed further later in this chapter (p 150).

Activities that facilitate group functioning

Group activities are an important resource in many courses and there is a large literature on them (Jaques, 1991). In this brief account, therefore, the emphasis is very much an encouragement to think about the purposes of the activities in relation to the anticipated outcome of the course. Group-work activities may also be the most likely area in which courses become misdirected into activities that serve, not the progress of the course towards having an impact on practice, but towards activities that satisfy only the comfortable functioning or development of the group. Alternatively, some group activities are played out like a ritual ('because that is what you do in short courses or groups'). Group work needs to support the progress towards the change of practice as well as any other purpose. We return to the important principle elucidated in Chapter 6, that good practice in instruction is related to the instructor being aware of the learner's state of understanding and needs. Too often group-work activities are imposed by a jaded instructor who enjoys her management better than the deployment of more subtle skills in facilitating learning. Group work might be said to have three different roles in a course:

- the knowledge and expertise of individuals in a group may be a valuable resource if it is tapped, valued and used as material of instruction;
- the quality of the functioning of a group can be a major issue in the quality of the environment for learning processes;
- group work is also a means of deepening learning (see later).

We discuss issues concerning the first two of the above in this section, not separating them because they overlap. The rationale for action in a course, however, does require that the distinction is understood. Some courses are conducted with little reliance on the group process, and with correspondingly heavy reliance on the material of instruction that is external to the participants. The extreme opposite of this is courses that rely largely on the initial expertise of those present. It is often the case that participants have sufficient knowledge (or can gain it for themselves) potentially in order to change their practice, but the knowledge is not appropriately organized and their confidence is not sufficiently developed in it for implementation. In the latter case, the expertise of the group could be the main learning resource used to encourage consolidation and organization of the knowledge base in relation to the proposed practice. However, it is not unusual for much time to be wasted in inefficient group work when some presentation of information would be helpful. Both have their place.

With a moderate number of people, groups that can work effectively together do not 'just happen'. Work needs to be done to support their functioning. Some of the initial activities that help participants to feel more 'group-orientated' are:

- effective introductions of participants and instructors;
- (sometimes) the building of a set of ground rules;
- games or exercises that are designed to ensure participant communication ('warm-up' exercises), to increase communication ('ice-breakers'), exercises that are designed to alter the attention level of the group, etc;
- work in small groups as well as in the plenary group;
- and so on.

While introductions and learning names can be important (Bourner, Martin and Race, 1993), they can also be a source of mistakes, and such mistakes matter more at the beginning of a course than later. For example, introductions can take an inordinate length of time in a large group, and hard-won attention can easily be lost. If people are asked to say something about themselves as well as their name, there is a tendency for more and more to be said as the task passes around the group. It is difficult to ask someone to stop talking when she is describing parts of her life that are important to her. Introductions in large groups need to be well considered first. Another way in which introductions can become a problem is when participants introduce each other and the details of the other are distorted or construed inaccurately.

It is not unusual at the introduction stage to ask people to describe an issue that they would like to be covered on the course. Apart from the time taken, this attempt at democracy can – as we have said earlier – become problematic when the timetable for the preset subject matter of the course is tight and a long list of new 'areas to be covered' emerges. The instructor either loses face or has to start excluding issues for fatuous reasons (instead of saying that there is not time available).

The development of a set of ground rules may or may not be important, depending on the nature of the course (whether, for example, confidentiality is important) and – as always – the relationship between such activity and the anticipated outcomes of the course. Ground rules, such as those concerning confidentiality, or the management of group discussion (Jaques, 1991) can be helpful in maintaining order and a sense of direction in a course. Bourner, Martin and Race (1992) suggest a set of ground rules. However, it is useful if the ground rules come from the group itself, so long as the exercise is seen as relevant to the course and is relatively quick and efficient.

There are many exercises or games that are used in learning groups. Some have purpose in themselves – a game might be used to give feedback on an activity and some are more generic. Among the 'objectives' for games, Kirby (1992) lists action planning, creativity, decision-making, elucidating expectations, development of listening skills, problem-solving, providing a mechanism for self-disclosure, increasing trust, and others. Perhaps, thinking in terms of objectives for games is the wrong way round. We should be thinking of the requirement for learning and then considering whether or not a game is the appropriate vehicle – or how an appropriate game should be devised.

Around 10 years ago games and exercises were new and refreshing but they can become a tedious repetition for those who have attended many courses, and then their tendency to be irrelevant to the purpose of the course becomes very evident. They run the danger of being seen as wasting time, and they can be a waste of time in terms of the anticipated outcome of the course. It is not difficult to devise relevant and purposeful games and exercises, particularly if prework has been done and the material is available. It is useful to use sources of group games and exercises, but to adapt them to the material of the course (eg Kirby, 1992). A useful exercise that is both good for facilitating group learning and for changing level of attention as well as helping in the integration of learning is 'quickthink' (p 148).

Another way of facilitating group function in order to improve learning in a course is to ask learners to work on subject matter in syndicate groups. A usual pattern is to ask someone in the group to record the work of the group and to feed back the outcomes to a later plenary session – theoretically so that everyone can benefit. While considerable learning might go on in the small groups as there is engagement in discussion, there is not often a sense of overall coherence. There are many factors that can reduce the value of this process:

- Small groups do not record as they discuss and do not remember what they have said.
- They scribble something down incoherently at the last moment (or when prompted).
- The person feeding back the material to the plenary did not write the notes and cannot read it – or does not have a good grasp of the ideas.

The value of asking the small groups to feed back their ideas to the plenary may be more to do with the summarizing within the small group, required as the material is prepared for feedback. On the other hand, if sufficient summarizing is not done, then the value of the feedback session is often dubious. The reasons for these failures can lie in the lack of clear instruction for the task or in the lack of discipline in following the instructions. If they do write directly on the flip-chart paper, the writing may not be clear enough to read – or, in particular, it is not processed sufficiently to be read – particularly when the reader is not the person who did the writing. It is valuable when setting up a group discussion exercise to stress that the group is responsible for the presentation of a flip chart that is a clear and legible account of their discussion.

Other considerations in terms of supporting the group are more concerned with the development of quality in the learning environment. There is a wider range of issues here that may extend out of what might be seen as 'course time'. The manner in which tea, coffee and lunch are served either encourages social interaction and discussion of course issues, or discourages them. In terms of overnight courses, placing a light course activity in the evening leaves participants with matters to discuss further at the bar. If there is a gap of days between parts of the course, setting up a discussion through e-mail can usefully facilitate contacts. The chances are that this will work better if there are actual issues presented for discussion – or if the discussion is about the participants' workplaces with reference to the proposed new practice. The section below on reflective activities suggests some ways of working with these times.

It is important to recognize that group formation processes can work against learning on a course. If there are issues that are unsatisfactory about a course, the development of groups may mean that a norm of grumbling develops among participants. For example, it is particularly important that any work that will be required outside the working hours of a course is declared beforehand. Setting up resentment at what might be construed as extra work is a mistake.

Activities to support the learner in implementing change in practice

It is worth anticipating practical difficulties that might occur in changing practice back in the workplace with appropriate action planning. This thinking may be reflective or more practical, using the expertise of the other course participants. For example, participants might be asked to spend a few minutes listing difficulties that they envisage in implementing the change in practice, and then framing some elements in the list into a statement about a problem that they will need to solve. In small groups (eg six in number), participants might each present their problems and use the group for discussion about solutions. Depending on the time available for this exercise, each has a set period of time for presenting the issue and the ensuing discussion. It can be useful if one of the group writes notes for each presenter and after the session, a 10-minute 'space' should be provided for everyone to write notes on what they have learnt – from their own and everyone else's discussions.

Another manner of supporting anticipated change in practice is to ask participants to write a list of impediments in their workplace environments to the implementation. This may be done as a group (brainstorming) or it may be an individual exercise, perhaps followed by a co-counselling session (p 154) on 'how I will overcome (some of) the impediments'.

A more elaborate means of thinking ahead about implementation of change is to ask participants to do a SWOT analysis of the envisaged changes. A SWOT analysis involves writing notes about the change in terms of its strengths, weaknesses, the opportunities that it presents and the threats that might dampen the opportunities. A SWOT analysis might precede the group exercise above.

Provision of overviews of the course – introductory or summarizing activities

Chapter 6 describes the need for the instructor of a course to have an overview of the content so that it is treated in a holistic manner, in order that the learner might gain a coherent view of it. It is important to convey to the learner the route by which the material included in the course leads to the envisaged change in practice (signposts, p 107). The introduction will also help the learner to see where emphases will be placed in the course. There are several ways in which this principle can be put into practice:

- through introductory activities in advance of the course;
- through introductory material;
- in summarizing activities.

The most obvious introductory activity in advance of a course is the detail of it, introducing the instructor and other information. This is an important opportunity to stress the ultimate aim of the course as improving impact on practice rather than just setting the details about the instruction itself. It is an opportunity to invite would-be participants to consider the implications for support in their workplace for changes that are envisaged.

Another means of addressing the content of the course in advance of it is by way of pre(course)work, (probably a series of several relevant questions to be answered), a copy of which is sent to the instructor before the course. The responses can then be used in the course. The framework described in Chapter 7 (p 126) may shape the kinds of questions that are useful to ask. So there might be questions about:

- the current practice with regard to the area of change;
- learning envisaged that will support the change;
- issues that might arise in implementing the change – or impediments to change;
- something about how things will be different when the change has been implemented.

In reality, it is often difficult to get potential participants to send in their work in advance and therefore there may not be much material with which to work. However, by asking for the material to be sent, at least it is then available to be designed into the ongoing work of the course. It is as well if the instructions for the prework indicate that it will take certainly no more than 20 minutes – five questions would be enough.

Prework generally means that learners have started to think of the subject matter of the course before they arrive and do not start from cold. It can be useful as a basis for 'warm-up' activities (see below). It may also form the first part of a course journal or reflective activities, which is continued within the course (p 150).

A variation on this form of prework, which also focuses on change in practice, is the requirement that the learner has a discussion about the proposed change in practice with a manager. The manager and the potential participant then sign to indicate that the meeting has occurred. This has a useful effect of bringing potential managerial support into the context of the course and the envisaged change.

Another form of introductory material other than the standard course introduction is the advance organizer (Ausubel, 1960). The idea of advance organizers has largely been applied to lesson-length instruction. It is a relatively short passage that introduces the session and which has the purpose of enabling learners mentally to organize their understanding of the ideas – recognizing, for example, how the new ideas link with previous ideas. Advance organizers might be used for the whole course and also as a means of introducing sessions in the course, always relating them to the envisaged change of practice.

Another way of introducing the sequence of a course is by way of a graphic depiction of its activities – envisaging the course as a journey on a road along which the learner travels (Rawlins, 1999). A further way of developing a coherent view of the learning in a course is through summarizing and debriefing activities. These may be programmed into the sequence of the course and given as part of the instruction, or they may be developed as exercises for the participants. Asking participants to summarize learning is a means of providing feedback to the instructor about the way in which participants have understood the course to that point. Summarizing may be verbal, but it might also be in graphic format – for example, as a concept map (p 149). Asking learners to draw their concept map for the learning on the course may well generate some valuable comments about understanding and lack of understanding among participants.

The process of debriefing may be more constructive than summarizing, though there are different perspectives on the meaning of the word, for example, Russell, 1994. Debriefing is a means of ensuring that the learner is able to make sense of a variety of ideas and observations, usually from experiential learning, so that learning may take place.

Activities to deepen or enable integration of learning

Both this and the next section (on reflective activities) are concerned with the deepening of learning, because that is an inevitable feature of the process of reflection (Moon, 1999). Many assessment procedures (p 157) have the same effect.

Chapter 3 emphasizes the importance of deep learning as opposed to surface learning (p 60) when the outcome of the learning is action and application. There are a number of activities suggested in these sections which may occur without input of information, or may follow provision of information. Quite often in professional development it is the case, however, that the participants do have most or all of the information needed, but may not have organized ideas about it. In this case, a session of brainstorming, or another method of pooling knowledge, might be followed by a session in which participants sort out their ideas by using one or more of the activities described below as a means of deepening their learning. Prework topics may be chosen with reference to subsequent activities in this area.

Questioning and discussion are common means of stimulating the deepening or integration of learning. While these activities occur in most courses, the manner in which they may or may not have an effect on the deepening of learning needs to be understood in order to manage them to their best advantage. Van Ments commented that '**discussion** must be one of the most widely used processes in education but is at the same time one of the most difficult of teaching procedures to use effectively. All too often the cry "Let's discuss that" is a signal for rambling aimless chat which fills time but achieves very little' (Van Ments, 1990, p 25). Van Ments suggests that part of the problem lies in the assumption that discussion is the same as conversation, an everyday occurrence. He defines discussion as 'a process whereby two or more people exchange information or ideas in a face-to-face situation to achieve a goal'(Van Ments, 1990, p 25). The achievement of a goal or conclusion is important. A conclusion is likely to signal to participants that something new has been learnt. There is a tendency in short courses and workshops to leave too many issues 'raised' but not concluded. Sometimes the 'conclusion' will be a summary of the session but at least it can provide the discussion with a sense of coherence.

It is also useful to go back to the constructs of deep and surface learning in order to further thought about discussion. The matter for consideration is how to manage the course situation in order that the learning is deep. Deep learning means that individuals will have a commitment to understanding, to making meaning, to linking the current ideas to previous ideas and knowledge.

The involvement of a deep approach to learning in order to achieve a conclusion to a discussion implies that some forethought is given to the structure of discussion sessions on short courses. Structure may be provided in the subject matter under discussion or in terms of the development of appropriate ways of behaving within the context of discussion. Debates provide structure in both the behaviour and the form of the subject matter and they are at the extreme of formalized discussions. Much less structure is provided in a well-considered question and open question (see below) or a requirement that a decision is made with justifications about a given issue (Moon, 1999).

Another form of structure may be in the form of ground rules for discussion, which may be decided by the participants. Van Ments suggests that some of the following may be useful:

- limit contributions to 30 seconds;
- wait 3 seconds after each contribution;
- no one speaks for a second time until everyone has spoken;
- 'time-outs' may be called at any time;
- and so on.

(Van Ments, 1990, pp 57–58)

Slightly different to ground rules, Abercrombie (1978) talks of the ways in which people need to learn to work with each other in discussion in order cooperatively to reach a goal that is a common advantage to all.

The facilitative use of **questions** is mentioned above. Questions can either prompt surface responses – like facts or 'yes/no' responses – or they can stimulate deep processing. Questions may play a part within an activity like discussion or they can be central to an activity in themselves. Morgan and Saxon (1991, pp 12–17) provide a useful classification of questioning that is based on the kinds of thinking processing that the questions demand. The categorization is as follows:

- questions that draw on knowledge (stimulate remembering, recognizing, defining, etc);
- questions that test comprehension (stimulating, interpreting, comparing, illustrating, explaining, rephrasing, etc);
- questions that require application (set up a problem to solve, require classifying, relating, hypothesizing, etc);
- questions that encourage analysis (require reasoning, the drawing of conclusions, taking a critical stance, inferring, etc);
- questions that invite synthesis (encourage creativity, combining, designing, developing, improving on, etc);
- questions that promote evaluation (encourage summarizing, assessing, arguing, reasoning, appraising, selecting and deciding priorities, etc).

Sometimes the simplest questions promote the most useful thinking at a deep level. '**Quickthink**' is a group activity that can usefully exploit this. Depending on the subject matter, it can fulfil a range of different purposes. A series of short questions (depending on the purpose for which the exercise is used) is collected on a sheet or an overhead projector slide. Participants are split into groups of three or four (no more for this) and are given a question. They have a short amount of time (eg three– five minutes) to develop an appropriate response. After the allocated time, groups are asked in turn to report either on the response, or on the ideas that contributed to it. Then another question is given. The questions can be humorous or everyday applications of principles that are the subject matter of the course. For example, in a course on writing learning outcomes for higher education modules, a quickthink question was: 'Write learning outcomes for a course on running parties for five-year-old children.'

   Another way in which learning can be deepened is by setting up a situation in which **participants are required to instruct each other**. In previous chapters several situations have been mentioned in which some participants in a short course may either know more about a specific topic than others, or are different in terms of readiness (Chapter 4) for the course. Generally speaking, to instruct another effectively requires that the instructor has a deep understanding of the material since the giving of explanation will draw on understanding.

Peer instruction may be used for a number of purposes. It could be used to transmit information, to enhance the understanding of those instructing, to enhance the understanding of those receiving instruction, or, where it is a mutual process and participants swap roles. There is benefit to all learners.

Sometimes peer instruction may be used to emphasize the differences between the way participants construe material of learning on the course or some area of prior knowledge or understanding. The use of **concept maps** can be helpful as a means of putting the structure of an idea on paper so that it can be examined by the originator herself and others. A concept map (Deshler, 1990) is a graphic depiction in which an idea is put in the centre of a page and associated ideas or developments of the original are placed on the page in relationship to the original (nearer or further from the it, in a branched structure, and so on). Having something on paper means that different views of the same idea are evident and that a discussion can ensue more easily.

Requiring participants to apply the new material of learning to different kinds of situations is another manner of deepening learning. The development of problems to solve using material of learning is a useful deepening technique. There is a range of **problem-solving** techniques that can be useful areas of learning for the participants (eg Schein, 1988, Robson, 1993) beyond the simplest situations. Similarly, a **critical incident** might be given to all of the participants to be analysed in terms of their new learning (Brookfield, 1990, Gayhe and Lillyman, 1997). A suitable critical incident might be a problem that is initially dealt with using the current workplace practice and then the new workplace practice. Alternatively, participants may develop typical critical incidents for each other.

Most methods of representation of learning can have the effect of deepening learning. What is important is that the instructor understands the nature of deep learning and its relationship to understanding and meaning, and is able to design the task so that learners cannot avoid processing the material by taking other than a deep approach.

Reflective activities

Reflection also deepens learning, but in this section we are focusing particularly on the role of reflection in enabling the learner to work through the phases of the framework to improve the impact of learning (Chapter 7, p 127). To summarize it, the framework consists of four phases. Phase 1 involves the development of awareness of the nature of current practice. Phase 2 consists of clarifying the new learning and considering how it relates to current understanding. Phase 3 concerns the integration of the new learning and current practice, and the issues for Phase 4 are the anticipation of the nature of the improved practice. A variety of techniques for reflection will serve to carry the learner through this sequence, and in this section we provide some examples. They may be more suitable for some phases than for others, or more suitable for use at the beginning of a course than towards the end. Much more information and many more examples of reflective activities are provided in Moon, 1999 and Moon, 1999a.

If reflective activity takes on an important role in a course, it is important to note that some participants will find it easier to reflect than others and their ability to reflect may not necessarily indicate their ability in other areas of the course. There is probably a tendency for instructors who reflect easily themselves to promote reflective activity and to assume that reflection comes as easily to others. This might be an issue when more than one instructor is involved in conducting a course, or when instructors have not designed the course that they conduct.

A means of maintaining a unifying thread through even a very short course is to ask participants to maintain a **learning journal or log** (Moon, 1999a). A learning journal is essentially a vehicle for reflection that will be written over a period of time and where generally the intention is one of learning. It may be structured or not. Here we are suggesting that some of the structure may be the phases of the framework that are listed above. In addition, reflective exercises can help learners to reflect more strategically or at a deeper level. However, most learners seem to appreciate the possibility of reflecting more freely (outside the structure of exercises) as well. When the course is a day long or shorter, the term 'learning log' may seem to be more appropriate. If prework is used (p 144), it can form the start of the learning log. The form of a log needs to be no more that loose-leaf pages attached together. In this way, prework or other exercises can be linked into other material very easily, and it can helpful if learners do not to know that they are writing a log until some of it is written. Also, in this form, the bare pages do not intimidate them.

A course learning log can be written in specially allocated pauses during the course, overnight, or in gaps between parts of a course (in a more-than-one-day course). Learners seem to appreciate short periods during which they can reflect on what they have learnt and how it relates to their work. The log may contain a variety of exercises or written work – including, perhaps, course notes. It is particularly useful if the log is continued beyond the course into the period during which practice is being improved or changed. However, unless the log is being assessed – or, at the least, reviewed by the instructor – some learners will not continue with it.

A learning log may be a means by which learners are assessed in a course since a log can create continuity between the work of the course and the period of time when the learning is implemented in the improvement of practice. Assessment of such material can be difficult in terms of the assessment criteria that are used and this is not made any easier when the assessment is a matter of passing or being not ready yet to pass. A major decision to make if logs are to be assessed is whether the product of the log in terms of the learning is important, or whether it is the development of the skills of reflection that are important. In the former case, a summative account such as a report, an essay or a presentation that is based on the log can provide an easier method of assessment. Some exercises that can structure reflective writing are given below. These may be part of a learning log or used alone. Some can form strands of similar activity that recur during a course.

Reflection can be encouraged in a structured manner by **carefully considered questions**. If the framework (p 127) is used, these are likely to be based on the four phases of the framework. They may use the wordings directly or indirectly. The questions might be given to learners at the beginning of the course as a whole and discussed in relation to the impact of the course on improvement or change in practice, and they are to be completed at different times. The time might be during the course or overnight and sometimes the completion of the reflection individually might be followed by a sharing of outcomes, which provides the instructor with the opportunity to relate the task to the framework again.

A variation on or addition to the giving of questions is to ask learners to **develop questions** relevant to the course or their practice or that they want to think further on themselves. This provides material for later exercises or discussion in the larger group, or they may use them in a co-counselling session (see below) or in a self-generated 'quickthink' session (p 148).

An alternative to the development of questions, is the statement of **problems or issues to solve** at the various stages of the framework and these might be resolved in the process of reflection. The problems or issues might emerge from, for example, a SWOT analysis (p 143). They might anticipate problems likely to emerge in the use of the new learning in practice.

Sometimes, the issues might concern work colleagues or managers or clients. Another way of encouraging reflection is to suggest that the issues involving others are expressed in 'letters' to be written but not sent. The use of '**unsent letters**' allows personal issues in practice to be explored and then usually tackled in practice in a more effectively assertive manner.

Another form of dealing with personal situations that impinge on the coursework or on the situation in practice is to work with **dialogue**. Dialogues are similar to scripts for plays in which the writer 'converses' with another (Moon, 1999a). The other could be those persons mentioned in the paragraph above, but might alternatively be inanimate – a project (for example, the course), an event (eg the subject matter of the critical incident study, p 149), or a task (eg implementing the proposed change). The other might be a social or religious influence or a mentor or person whose advice is valued, or something/somebody imagined. Most people will find dialogues initially easier when the other is a person, but can gain interesting insights from dialogues with inanimate 'others'. When writing in this mode, unexpected but helpful ideas can emerge. The technique involves simply writing one's position, perhaps greeting the other and then 'seeing' what comes into mind about what the other has to say – and recording it and responding – or perhaps sometimes asking a question.

A technique that accords well with the structure of the framework is '**currere**' that was originally developed by Pinar (1975) in connection with work on the school curriculum. It involves taking a particular topic and reflecting on it in its present context, then in its past context and then on how it might be in the future. Grumet (1987) suggests that 'multiple accounts splinter the dogmatism of a single tale. If they undermine the authority of the teller [they] also free her from being captured by the reflection provided in a single narrative'. A variation on currere is writing an account of the process of improving and changing practice – **a rehearsal**. This may demonstrate some unexpected issues. This reflective exercise would be usefully followed up by work with a 'critical friend' (see below) who could ask further questions.

There are many exercises that are graphic, rather than verbal. The **road or route map** exercise is a useful example. The participants are asked to draw a route map or, for example, their career (or the elements of career relevant to the subject matter of the course). Route maps show obstacles (hills, mountains, narrow roads), branches, times where ideas have flowed (eg downhill), very satisfying times (beautiful landscape), etc. The routes might extend into the near future. On a smaller scale, the route/road map might concern the learning in the course itself and then it might deliberately refer to the phases of the framework. Exercises such as this suggest new areas to consider, but they do need to be followed up so that the emergent ideas are recognized and they can become food for more thought, then related to the flow of learning towards the anticipated learning outcomes.

A model of reflection that encourages deeper reflection on initial reflection is the **double entry** journal. Here the initial ideas are explored on one side of a page (or on one page) and later the material is subjected to further reflection, perhaps in more depth, or perhaps in a broader context on the opposite (side of the) page.

Co-counselling and the development of a system of critical friends are ways of enhancing and deepening the reflective work. **Co-counselling** involves two participants working together. Initially one has a period of time to explore a topic orally, supported by the other who might facilitate the exploration but does not impose her agenda on it. Her main role is to listen actively. Then this reverses and the other is listened to. Co-counselling might be used before a period of personal reflective writing or after it, or just to explore personal orientations to areas of subject matter.

A critical friend acts differently. She does not just listen, but, working on the reflections (verbal or oral) of another, seeks to probe, query and ask deeper questions so that the value of the reflective exercise is increased. A system of critical friends may be set up at the start of a course or used in one-off sessions after periods of reflection. Some practice may be needed by participants in order to operate successfully and helpfully. For example, the provision of feedback to the critical friend as to how facilitative she has been may be useful.

Activities to support individual learning or coping behaviours

A number of times in this book, we have suggested that an issue in many short courses is the fact that those who participate start the course with very different abilities, experiences, and states of readiness for the subject matter. Depending on the aim or outcomes of the course this may or may not be a problem. Additionally, the work settings in which the new or improved practice may take place may differ. These factors may mean that some level of individual support is provided for all or for just some of the participants and this may function only during the course – or during and after the course – or perhaps before the course as well. There is a variety of ways of managing the need for individual support depending on the resources and what the learning on the course is intended to achieve:

- The development of a tutorial system so that learners are seen individually at some stage in the course – the rest of the group may be engaged in some independent work that has a diagnostic element, providing information about weaknesses for the tutorial sessions. Designing a situation in which some time can be spent with individuals (or carefully considered pairs or threes) can be important even in very short courses.
- Extra coaching or support is arranged in the workplace for those whose learning shows deficits.
- Use of peers – while some learners may be struggling, it is likely that others are ahead of the course in their skills as learners or in their learning towards the learning outcomes. Peer support may be arranged in an overt manner, or it may be a matter of ensuring that small groups are set up to focus on the topics of difficulty, with each group containing learners with strengths and weaknesses.
- Concept mapping in groups (p 149) – if a group is asked to develop concept maps, it is likely that those who understand the concepts best will dominate, enabling those who understand less well to learn from their peers. The instructor will need to ensure that the group map is appropriately drawn, or that there is support for the group as a whole to draw a more appropriate version.
- In a similar way, groups could be asked to provide a summary of the previous session.
- Action learning groups are a less managed version of the point above.

We have suggested before that sometimes there is wide span of expertise and experience in learning in a group of people who are enrolled on a short course. The instructor may or may not be aware of where deficits lie in relation to the learning outcomes of the course because she may never have met the participants before. Finding the best starting point can be difficult. The best starting point will be one that does not leave some participants irretrievably behind and equally that does not cause a sense of wasted time in others. Sometimes at the beginning of a course, decisions have to be made extremely quickly.

It may be possible to run a system of **tutorials** within the course. These could be for all the participants or just those who are having difficulties. The difficulty might be in participants envisaging how they can improve their practice, rather than specifically academic difficulty. Tutorial systems might benefit from the presence of a second instructor or tutor for the course who is familiar with the participants' needs. It will be important, however, to ensure that learners do not miss any important work while they are withdrawn for their sessions though tutorial sessions, which could, perhaps, continue after the end of the course and could constitute a general support meeting for all who have been involved. Ensuring that participants meet again beyond the end of the course is an incentive for them to implement the practice so that they have something to report in the later meeting. Such a meeting might be linked with assessment procedures (p 157).

There are alternative ways of getting around a variety of differences in participants. There may be expertise within the group of participants and either judicious pairings or the development of small expert-led participant-run groups to enable **peer support** may suffice without the need to make extra arrangements. A variation on peer support is the use of critical friends (p 154) where the 'friend' is selected for her expertise and the reciprocity is managed in a different way. A further variation that will work on a longer short course is to set up a buddy system from the start, or before the start. Buddies might be linked on the basis of similar workplaces or similar issues in improving practice. An important element in such a system would be the continuity of contact after the end of the course so that the mutual support continues. Buddies could, of course, be in small groups rather than in pairings. The sharing of e-mail addresses/phone numbers at an early stage is important for these arrangements.

Probably the most helpful form of support for participants on a course who are expected to improve workplace practice is the development of a system in which there is support from those actually in the workplace. Many of the problems of implementing change in practice emanate from the workplace and direct involvement of the workplace is obviously advantageous. Ideally the **mentor** would have interests in the same area and would be in contact with the course participant before the course as well as supporting her during and after it.

The provision of individual support may relate to assessment tasks. They may provide the opportunity to discuss the learner's progress in relation to her performance on an assessed task (see below). The provision of feedback (see below) on a short course requires care because of the limited time and the sensitivity that is often involved. An individual's learning could be disrupted for the remainder of the course if she is upset by feedback given insensitively. Similar issues apply when feedback is given in a group situation (Russell, 1994).

Sometimes the reason for working with individuals separately on a course is because of difficult behaviour. There is a range of behaviours that can both disrupt the learning of the individual or, more significantly, that of other participants. Some of the difficulties might be in learning (skills or knowledge) or in the attitudes to the course. Talkativeness can be difficult to handle, as can the 'compulsive answerer', the 'I don't want to be here' learner, the lost and confused, the angry or aggressive, the quiet person, the know-it-all, and so on (Clothier, 1996). Sometimes, then, using the techniques of one-to-one work might be more appropriate.

Assessment activities to evaluate personal learning

By assessment we mean the consideration of the results of individual learning. The section after this one concerns evaluation, by which we mean the judgement of the success of the course as a whole. While this might concern the quality of the learning or change or improvement of practice, equally it might concern the administration procedures and the ways in which they could be improved on for a later course.

There are many purposes for which assessment is used other than simply to attribute a mark that indicates quality of performance. Assessing work allows for various forms of feedback information. It provides feedback for the learner on her performance; it provides an indication of the quality of the instruction for the instructor; and it enables the instructor to provide the learner with feedback.

Assessment might also indicate to the learner whether her learning is sufficient for progression to a further stage in learning. Depending on the purpose for assessment, assessment criteria may or may not relate to the learning outcomes and assessment criteria identified at the beginning of a course. If assessment concerns the quality of the overall learning on the course, then it needs to measure the learning that is described in the learning outcomes. As we have described in Chapter 1, these may relate to the learning on the course only or the outcome of change or improvement in practice at the end of the course.

One of the main effects of assessment in a short course, is that it is likely to improve learning. There is a danger that learners on an unassessed course simply sit through it and do not integrate the ideas in it with their current practice or with the target of improvement in practice. Perhaps one of the assumptions that tends to be made about assessment is that it is always formal and the degree of excellence is the main issue. Assessment may be informal and may be primarily in place to provide feedback and to improve learning. We have mentioned the work of Angelo and Cross (1990) who provide many examples of 'classroom assessment techniques' (CATS) that are designed to facilitate learning in this way. Many of these techniques are extremely simple and provide the instructor with valuable information. It is important to consider how the nature of anticipated assessment relates to the manner in which learners learn. Chapter 3 describes approaches to learning that are deep and surface. There is plenty of evidence that a learner's belief about the demands of an assessment task can influence the approach to learning that she will adopt. It is possible to envisage a situation in an assessed short course where the task is perceived by learners to need a surface approach to learning when they need to take a deep approach in order to implement improvement or change in practice. It is, therefore, important not only that the task is in accordance with the learning outcomes and the ultimate change in practice, but that it is also encouraging the appropriate form of learning. There is, for example, a tendency for learners to associate multiple choice questions with the need to know facts and sometimes figures, rather than to understand the material (Trigwell and Prosser, 1999). This could be at odds with the need to apply understanding to a change in practice. It is important to remember that, in this way, assessment can drive learning and it can drive it in the wrong way or the appropriate way. Instruction that will lead to appropriate learning needs the use of techniques of assessment that indicate the understanding of the learners (Trigwell and Prosser, 1999).

Assessment tasks should be chosen in relation to the kinds of learning that is required, and the learning outcomes for the course. They may or may not bear direct relevance to the nature of the practice. Some assessment tasks might include:

- responses to short questions;
- role play;
- presentations;
- essays;
- projects;
- reviews of the literature on particular issue;
- course logs or journals (p 150);
- reports on/evaluation of the changed practice;
- research projects;
- written reports of assessment of need for change in relation to participant's practice;
- reflection on or reports on aspects of the workplace in relation to the anticipated change in practice;
- written accounts of practical work;
- responses to a quiz;
- and so on.

It is important in a short course, where participants' experience of assessment processes might be variable, that the demands of the task itself (eg the actual writing of a report) do not become more difficult than the representation of the learning itself. It is appropriate that the assessment criteria for the work are produced in advance and are used to guide learners so that they know the kind of work that is expected, and so, also, that their perceptions of the requirements guide their learning appropriately.

Course evaluation activities

The evaluation of a course is the process of exploring how a course 'has affected the individual participants, the work they are doing and, possibly, the organization within which they are working' (HEA, HEBS, HPW, HPANI, 1995). The purpose of evaluation usually contributes to decisions about further courses or learning activities. Unfortunately there can be a tendency for evaluation to be tagged on to the end of courses rather than being seen as an integral part of the design. Depending on decisions made during planning, the evaluation activities associated with a course may go well beyond the course itself. Questions may be asked of the managers of those involved in the course, or the participants themselves, of their clients and colleagues, the instructors involved and so on. Here are some examples of the aspects of a course that might be evaluated:

Before the course
● the match of the aims and learning outcomes to training needs of participants;
● match of the aims and learning outcomes to course structure;
● the match of the aims and learning outcomes to content (components) of the course;
● the relationship of the learning outcomes of the course to the anticipated impact of the learning in the workplace practice;
● the competency of the instructors to facilitate the learning to the learning outcomes.

During the course
● the degree to which aims and learning outcomes are being met;
● the process of the course in terms of enjoyment and general satisfaction for the participants;
● the process of the course in terms of enjoyment and general satisfaction for the instructors.

Immediately after the course
● the degree to which course learning outcomes have been met;
● the anticipated effectiveness of the transfer of course learning to the work situation;

- the effectiveness of the administrative processes;
- immediate indications of the needs for further learning for participants.

A predetermined longer time after the course
- assessment of the impact of the course on workplace practice (anticipated change or improvement);
- the effect of the course on the organization(s) of the participants;
- the effectiveness of the course as perceived by the immediate managers of participants on the course;
- the wider perceptions of the course by all of those involved;
- the identification of those who benefited from the course;
- the cost-benefit or effectiveness of the courses;
- indications of the need for further learning;
- and so on.

This range of different factors indicates that there could be a variety of different means of evaluating a course. Most usual are those methods that involve course participants completing a questionnaire given out just before they depart – often at the point where they are thinking of the train times and where their car keys are. These questionnaires will clearly provide information for those running the course rather than information that is directly to the benefit of the participants. Another form of evaluation involves the ongoing monitoring of how the course is going in terms of participants' learning and their general satisfaction. Below are a variety of evaluation tools that can fulfil different purposes.

In terms of the more detailed information of the course, the **questionnaire** can involve closed questions (yes/no) or open-ended questions that are more difficult to summarize. A variation on the preset questionnaire that can elicit very useful information is to ask participants '**if you were designing this evaluation on what issues would you focus?**' This can be developed into a useful exercise where the issues on which the course should be evaluated are developed, and then used as a basis for response.

Process observation may be useful for providing detailed information about particular activities during a course. A participant or a second instructor acts as an observer and records appropriate detail about the processes that are occurring in the course at the time. The material will need to be summarized, but an observation schedule may help. More detailed information may be obtained from anyone involved in a course by organizing **focus groups** after the course.

More informal information about how the course is going for learners can be obtained from a variety of quick and easy exercises. For example, learners may be asked to sum up their feelings about an activity of part of the course by giving **a summary in three words**. Slightly more blunt is a '**thumbs up/thumbs down**' sign. They might be asked for '**three things that you will take away from today**' that will help you in your practice. A variation on this is to ask participants how they would **market the course** – what they would tell other people about it to encourage them to come. What would they not tell them?

An exercise that requires slightly more forethought is **the tree exercise**. Participants are given a photocopy of a simply drawn tree on an A4 sheet and they are asked to draw themselves on the tree to depict the state of their learning on/satisfaction with the course. A variation is a tree with drawings of people already on it at various heights and states of confidence and competence in their climb and the learners are asked to circle the person who looks most like the way that they feel at the current stage in the course. Another variation is one in which one large tree is drawn and participants draw themselves on yellow sticky 'Post-its' and place these in their chosen positions on the tree. Another 'Post-its' exercise is to place a **chart on the wall** to receive comments on 'Post-its' – though they can be directly written as well.

A further source of information about how courses have worked for learners can be **learning logs or journals**. The use of the journal for evaluative material may be explicit and may be based on an evaluation task, or journals may be reviewed for their more general comments about the course.

9

Improving the impact of short courses: a summary of the main ideas

Introduction

This chapter pulls together the main ideas that have emerged in the chapters of this book. It is not a summary of all of the content, but a repeat of the important ideas. It can act as a synopsis for rapid reading or it may serve more practical purposes as a quick reference or checklist for those who are using the book alongside work with courses.

Aims and learning outcomes (Chapter 1)

When developing a course or when checking it for review or accreditation purposes, it is worth following a sequence of factors that are components of the design of a course. Structuring factors influence the nature, quality, or content of a course and they will be reflected in the course aims and learning outcomes. Some of the main sources of structuring factors include:

- continuing professional development requirements (eg professional body standards that provide license to practice);

- factors that determine standards (eg descriptions of levels in higher education; national vocational qualifications);
- curriculum and the desire to inform or share interest (eg concern to express the content of a curriculum);
- identified training needs (identified by the learner or others).

There is often confusion about the differences between aims, object-ives and learning outcomes. The differences between aims and learning outcomes relate to the differences between the process of teaching and that of learning:

- An aim is an expression of teaching intention – what will be covered on the course.
- A learning outcome is an expression of what it is intended that a learner will have learnt at the end of a course.
- An objective can be written in terms of teaching intention or intended learning and therefore the use of the term can cause confusion.

In terms of definition, within the teaching intention, an aim often expresses an introductory statement to a course. It might refer to prerequisite knowledge or the rationale for the course. A learning outcome is an expression of what a learner is expected to know, understand, or be able to do at the end of the course. There are many justifications for writing learning outcome statements for courses:

- They give direction and purpose to learning on a course.
- They provide a guide for instruction on a course.
- They make it possible to determine when required learning has been achieved on a course.
- They provide information about the course to participants, their managers and others.
- They can provide a record of what has been achieved in a course (eg for a portfolio);
- and so on.

A learning outcome should usually have three components:

- a verb showing on what the learner is acting;
- an indication of what the learner is learning (the object of the verb);
- an indication of the standard (in terms of context or standard) of the performance required to demonstrate that the learning has been achieved.

Learning outcomes may be written for the end of the duration of the course, or for the demonstration of the learning in workplace practice (impact) or both.

Assessment criteria are statements of what the learner will need to do either to indicate that she has reached threshold standard in the course (threshold assessment criteria), or that she has learnt sufficient to be awarded a particular grade (grade assessment criteria). Assessment criteria may be closely related to the learning outcome (particularly the third part of the outcome statement) or to the task itself. In the latter case, they should relate also to the learning outcome statement.

Learning on short courses (Chapters 2, 3, and 4)

Teaching, instructing and learning are separate activities, but in the literature and in common parlance there are frequent confusions between them. The lack of distinction between the words may result in the making of unwarranted assumptions about the intentions of learners and may mean that initiatives in instruction are assumed explicitly or implicitly to have a direct influence on what the learner learns.

One reason for the confusions that exist between instruction and learning is that there are 'gaps' in the vocabulary. New terms are proposed:

- material of learning – that which is learnt by the learner;
- material of instruction or teaching – that which is taught by the teacher;

- the representation of learning – the learner's expression of whatever she has learnt in formal assessed situations or in practice;
- learning challenge – the relative challenge that a given piece of learning sets up for a specific learner in a given context.

If the material of instruction and the material of learning are seen as coinciding, then the instructor might need to find out what the learner knows already, but beyond that the process of instruction is simply to add to what is known. If an instructor works on the premise that the material of learning and the material of instruction are different, then she can devise various means of working towards bringing them into greater alignment if required. Some instruction is oriented towards stimulating the learner to think in a divergent manner, exploring ideas and going beyond the information that is given. Then it is desirable that the material of learning is made to differ from that of instruction. The material of instruction then sets up a learning challenge for the learner.

There are differences in views of learning in different educational cultures and in the histories of those cultures. Short courses have a place within cultures of training, academic and adult education and in the context of this book, therefore, we work all three views of learning. Individuals also have different views of learning. An exploration of metaphors for learning demonstrates a considerable variation.

If the learner's concept of learning will affect the manner in which she learns, the existence of different views of learning from within the different educational cultures and among individuals is highly significant. This is particularly important as the boundaries between, for example, higher education and commerce and industry are crossed in such initiatives as lifelong learning. The significance of different views of learning and the learner extend to instruction since the instructor's view of learning influences her manner of instruction.

There are many theories of learning, some of which, like the cycle of experiential learning, dominate particular educational cultures. Theories tend to be presented as if they explain the totality of learning. Most probably have some explanatory or descriptive value, but it is limited to aspects of the learning process or particular contexts.

In relation to the points made above, a theory of learning will tend to be based on a particular view of the learner. It is important to recognize this in using the theory. Theory is a manner in which thinking about learning is organized. The general stance taken is that theories of learning are to be used like tools – used only where they are useful – and it is unlikely that any one tool is adequate alone or that any one tool will serve all purposes. There are particular characteristics of learning on short courses:

- There tends to be an intention that something is done differently as a result of the course.
- Time on the course is short and the learning is concentrated.
- Short courses can provide intellectual space for thinking about work practices. However, it is often the case that because they are concentrated, they do not provide enough time and opportunity for reflection.
- Good quality learning that is to be applied is not a tidy process. Learning that is too 'tidy' and 'prepackaged' is often not appropriate, and yet the nature of the short course will often encourage instructors or course managers to adopt such a view of learning in designing their instruction methods.
- There are characteristics of a short course *per se* that influence learning, eg the shortness, that learning is concentrated, learner motivation, the 'tidiness' or 'messiness' of the learning.

The context of a short course affects the nature of the learning that is likely to occur. It is important to be aware of the effects for the learners and to relate it to the type of learning that is required in order for the course to have impact on practice. Eraut's model of professional learning provides a useful framework for consideration of the subject matter of short courses. It describes propositional knowledge (theory); personal knowledge and the sense made of experience and process knowledge. Espoused knowledge does not necessarily guide practice. As a practitioner becomes more experienced she will develop 'theories-in-use', deriving her practice from these ideas. Practitioners may find it difficult to articulate their theories-in-use (which equate to Eraut's third type of knowledge, personal knowledge). Short courses may deal with any of the forms of learning and knowledge identified by Eraut. It is important to recognize the role of theories-in-use and to encourage their articulation. Once explicit the theories are amenable to review and possible modification.

Learning from experience is particularly important and influential in the literature of training. There tends to be a notion that experiential learning is always 'better' than 'being told'. The paradigms on which experiential learning is based are somewhat vague. The Kolb cycle of experiential learning is often presented as the process of learning but it should be subject to questioning (Kolb, 1984). For example:

- What is the nature of relevant 'experience'?
- In the cycle, does 'reflective observation' come before learning (abstract conceptualization) or is it what we do when we work with what we have already learnt?
- Does the cycle describe learning or a process of guiding learning (in effect, instruction)?

Learning occurs within an environment that affects the learning process. A systems approach to the learning environment includes factors within the immediate environment of the learner, the ethos of the organization or institution, instructors and the process of instructing, the social environment and anything else. Anything can affect learning, depending on the viewpoint of the learner and the manner in which she perceives the object. In logical terms it is not possible to predict how a learner will react to any given environment effect. In practice some guesswork is appropriate.

The principle of limiting factors adds to our understanding of how a learning environment might work. A limiting factor is an environmental factor that is at the limits of the learner's tolerance. The principle helpfully suggests that what might normally be a limiting factor can be modified in its action by the presence of another factor. In other words, environmental factors interact to reduce the predictability of their effects. The social environment acts no differently to the physical environment. However, the presence of a group of people may be exploited to produce advantages in the learning process of participants.

Chapter 3 explores qualities of learning in terms of depth, meaning and complexity in learning. The words 'knowledge' and 'understanding' imply different qualities of learning. Differences between these qualities are directly related to the manner in which people function in representing the learning – for example, in workplace activity. Coherence and the development of meaning from learning are evidenced in the ways in which learning is represented. Poor learning is represented in an unstructured manner, with points unrelated or poorly related. It is associated with a surface approach to learning. Good quality learning is represented in a more holistic manner, is coherent and appropriately structured. It is associated with a deep approach to learning.

Understanding that there are different qualities to learning enables courses to be designed appropriately and efficiently towards the quality that is required. The understanding will also enable instructors to operate in a manner to facilitate the required depth of learning. Deep, surface and strategic approaches to learning have been identified. A deep approach occurs where the learner is engaged with the meaning of the learning. A surface approach occurs where the learner simply tries to memorize the material without relating it to previous material or trying to understand its meaning. A strategic approach occurs where the learner deploys whatever approach is necessary to achieve her purpose (eg pass an assessed task or please a manager). Learning that will have an impact on practice will probably need to be deep learning. If this is the case, then the structure of a short course and the instruction processes should be such to encourage learners to take a deep approach to learning.

A constructivist view of learning suggests that the learner construes learning according to her prior knowledge and understanding. An implication of this is that meaning is developed by the learner.

The cognitive structure represents what is known or understood by the learner. In learning something new, two processes occur. The material of learning is taken in (assimilated) and the cognitive structure modifies itself in response to the new learning (accommodation). The cognitive structure (what is already known and understood by the learner) guides the process of assimilation of new material of learning.

There are many implications of this for both learning and instruction. If meaning is that which is understood by the learner, it cannot be truly objectively assessed. An instructor has to do her best to gauge the meaning that a learner has constructed. Another implication is that the learner is in charge. The learner can decide how much she will allow her cognitive structure to modify in response to new material of learning. She may be open to new ideas or resistant. Many variables will affect this, including constitutional factors and such matters as the credibility of the source of information.

The map of learning and the representation of learning are attempts to draw together a range of ideas about the process of learning, the qualities of learning and respective outcomes of learning. It hypothesizes quality of learning as a series of stages of learning that progressively process learning in a more sophisticated manner, thus generating increasing levels of meaning

It is suggested that surface (memorized) learning can be 'upgraded' or deepened through opportunities for increasing understanding and relating the new material of learning to what is known already. Further learning also occurs when learning is represented. When a learner, for example, writes about something that she has learnt, she is learning more about it and probably deepening the learning at the same time.

The rationale for learning from experience is explained by these references to upgrading learning and learning from the representation of learning. By having to represent learning in an active manner, the learner is forced to adopt a deep approach to learning. Secondly, because the learning is represented, there is an opportunity for further learning to occur. In this way, the operation of the Kolb cycle is explained in the map of learning and the representation of learning.

Chapter 4 is concerned with variables associated with the learner herself. Most of these variables would appear to operate in influencing the approach that the learner adopts to the learning, or in determining the complexity of information with which the learner can deal. Learners attend a course with a prior orientation – a set of attitudes, aims and purposes for learning. The research of Beaty, Gibbs and Morgan (1997) suggests that the orientations of higher education students include vocational, academic, personal and social aspects. The learner's orientations to the course will determine the approach that she adopts to learning on it. Many short courses are delivered in the context of professional development. On a short course there may be participants who are at different stages of their professional development, but who are involved in the same area of work. A factor that may influence a learner's orientation to a course might be their stage of professional development. The implication of this research is that the learner's orientation will affect the manner in which she approaches the learning on a course. Some learners do not attend courses for the reason that they personally are interested in the learning opportunity.

Learners may vary in their readiness for a course, depending on the learning challenges that face them. Some may not be sufficiently independent; some may not understand how to reflect on and learn from their own experiences. Similarly, learners may be well or less well prepared for a course in emotional terms. Participants on a short course may arrive with a variety of reactions to it – from those who are self-motivated to those who have been sent to learn something about which they are unenthusiastic.

There are many ways in which learners vary and there is much research to support different constructs to describe differences. There are learning styles, strategies and intelligence(s). While much research has been done, there are relatively few reliable findings – perhaps partly because the constructs overlap but also because learners compensate for weaknesses in one aspect of the learning process with strengths in others.

Another area of individual difference would seem to be in the quality of thinking of the learner. Several studies have shown evidence of different stages of thinking which concern, for example, the ability to manage uncertainty and the understanding that knowledge is constructed by the learner.

Dealing with all of these issues of individual difference can pose problems for those running short courses. There are limits to the diversity of learners with which an instructor on a course can usefully cope. Using the experience and abilities among the participants to help those who are weaker is a possible strategy.

Instruction in short courses (Chapters 5, 6)

Chapters 5 and 6 are based on the content of the chapters on learning because good instruction takes account of the learning of learners. It is a tenet of this book that learners will make sense of learning in their own way and therefore good instruction should monitor the learning process in order to guide learning in the directions of the learning outcomes required on the course. Not all instruction is viewed in this way. As with the conceptions of learning, there are different conceptions of the process of instruction and some are more helpful for learners than others. Conceptions of learning (from Fox, 1983) include:

- Shaping theories, where the instructor shapes the learning of the learner.
- Transfer theories that consider that the knowledge of the instructor is passed to the learner.
- Travelling theories that put the instructor in the role of a guide to the learner on her learning 'journey'.
- Growing theories, where the learner's mind is nurtured by the provision of an appropriate environment.

Trigwell and Prosser (1999) found that learners learnt more meaningfully from instructors who focus on the learning of learners rather than those who focus on their own activities of instruction. In other words, focus on the learning is more likely to encourage a deep approach to learning among learners. However, there are no 'right ways to teach'. Earlier chapters have indicated that there are many variables that affect a learner's approach to learning, and the approach may change during a course. An instructor needs to be aware of, and responsive to, changes in the learning of the participants, particularly when time is short on a short course. She continually needs to be relating these to the learning outcomes and notions of changes in workplace practice.

Chapter 6 considers a number of features of instruction that will encourage learners to adopt a deep approach to their learning. The features of instruction are listed below with brief notes:

- Working with a holistic view of the course and its structure means that those who instruct should have an overview of the course, understanding how the elements in the course fit together. They should 'signpost' the course for learners so that they know where they are, and how the elements work towards the content of learning outcomes and/or change in their practice. A good instructor will have a sense of ownership of the material of instruction in the course.
- The management of the balance of time and workload means that time and workload can be considered in relation to the intended goal(s) of the course – the learning outcomes, and the anticipated change in practice. Aspects of this are:
  - sufficiency of overall time to reach the goals;
  - a workload for participants that enables them sufficient time for required learning;
  - pacing of instruction that takes account of the learning of participants;
  - intellectual space – adequate time for reflection, particularly in relation to the meaning involved in taking a deep approach to learning;
  - adequate account of 'wait time' that concerns the pacing of instruction.
- The management of a positive emotional climate can facilitate learning or, if mismanaged, can severely disrupt it. As with many other aspects of good-quality instruction, it is a matter of awareness of this dimension on the part of the instructor – and the ability to respond appropriately.
- Good management of the attention of learners is probably a prerequisite for the progress of their learning towards attainment of specified learning outcomes, or change in practice. If their attention does not matter, there is something wrong with the structure of the programme. As above, instructors need to be aware of learner attention and able to respond appropriately.
- Good management of the depth of learning and encouragement of a deep approach to learning include:
  - enabling learners to know what they are expected to learn and how they will know when they have learnt it;
  - monitoring the processes of learning among participants;

- requiring learners to represent their learning;
- enabling them to develop a sense of ownership of their learning;
- challenging learners so that they have to think about what they are doing;
- enabling learners to develop awareness of their own learning process.
- monitoring the progress of learning – the instructor needs to know if learning is progressing appropriately but this does not necessarily mean that there should be formal assessment. There are many quick methods of finding out whether learning is satisfactory.

While it is important to facilitate the learning of individual course participants, there is also a need to pay attention to the progress of the whole group and facilitate a movement of all towards the learning outcomes and impact anticipated. This means that there is a need to take account of those who might be having more difficulties – either with the learning or because they have started the course with some disadvantage.

There are also technical skills in instruction that can supersede all of the references to facilitating deep learning above. The technical skills include:

- use of voice;
- conveyance of credibility;
- clear explanation and presentation;
- organization of the instruction;
- display of enthusiasm for the subject matter of the course.

Designing courses for impact (Chapter 7)

In Chapter 7, a framework is developed that can be used in a number of ways to design or structure short courses. It is based on the idea that in order to change practice, it is important that course participants are aware of the nature of their current practice with respect to the area of potential change. Such practice is often tacit. The framework to improve the impact of learning in short courses follows the following phases:

- developing awareness of the nature of current practice;
- clarifying the new learning and how it relates to current under-standing;
- integrating new learning and current practice;
- anticipating or imagining the nature of improved practice.

This framework provides a useful structure for reflective work.

Components of courses (Chapter 8)

Components of courses are groups of activities that have a common purpose in a course. Actual activities may fit a number of components depending on the purposes for which they are used. Since the text that describes each component is clear in Chapter 8, just the titles of the component elements are listed below:

- course planning or administrative activities;
- activities that involve actual instruction or the delivery of information;
- activities that facilitate group functioning to improve the learning resource of the group and the learning environment;
- activities to support the learner in implementing change in practice;
- provision of overviews of the course – introductory or summa-rizing activities;
- activities to deepen or enable integration of learning (other than reflective activities);
- reflective activities;
- activities to support individual learning or coping behaviours;
- assessment activities to evaluate personal learning;
- course evaluation activities.

References

Abercrombie, M (1979) *Aims and Techniques of Group Teaching*, 4th edn, SRHE, London

Angelo,T and Cross, K (1990) *Classroom Assessment Techniques*, Jossey-Bass, San Francisco

Ausubel, D (1960) 'The use of advance organisers in the learning and retention of meaningful verbal material', *Journal of Educational Psychology*, **51**, pp 267–72

Ausubel, D and Robinson, F (1969) *School Learning*, Holt, Rhinehart and Winston, London

Barnett, R (1997) *Higher Education, a Critical Business*, SRHE/OUP, Buckingham

Beaty, E, Gibbs, G and Morgan, A (1997) 'Learning orientation and study contracts' in *The Experience of Learning,* eds F Marton, D Hounsell and N Entwistle, Scottish Academic Press

Belenky, M, Clinchy, B, Goldberger, R and Tarule, J (1986) *Women's Ways of Knowing*, Basic Books, New York

Bermann-Brown, R (1994) 'The Language of knowing and learning: bridging the apparent dichotomies' in *Improving Student Learning*, ed G Gibbs, OCSLD, Oxford Brookes University, Oxford

Biggs, J (1993) From theory to practice, a cognitive systems approach, *HE Research and Development*, **12**, pp 73–85

Biggs, J (1999) *Teaching for Quality Learning at University*, SRHE/OUP, Buckingham

Biggs, J and Collis, K (1982), *Evaluating the Quality of Learning*, Academic Press, New York

Bloom, B (1956) *Taxonomy of Educational Objectives: the cognitive domain*, David McKay, New York

Boud, D, Keogh, R and Walker, D (eds) (1985) *Reflection, Turning Experience into Learning*, Kogan Page, London

Bourner, T, Martin, V and Race, P (1993) *Workshops that Work*, McGraw-Hill International (UK) Ltd, Maidenhead, Bucks

Brockbank, A and McGill, I (1998) *Facilitating Reflective Learning in Higher Education*, SRHE/OUP, Buckingham

Brookfield, S (1990) 'Using critical incidents to explore assumptions' in *Fostering Critical Reflection in Adulthood*, ed J Mezirow, Jossey-Bass, San Francisco

Brown, G (1978) *Lecturing and Explaining*, Methuen, London

Brown, G and Atkins, M (1997) *Effective Learning in Higher Education*, Routledge, London

Burnard, P (1991) *Experiential Learning in Action*, Avebury Press, Aldershot

Candy, P, Harri-Augstein, S and Thomas, L (1985) 'Reflection and the self-organised learner: a model of learning conversations in *Reflection: Turning experience into learning*, D Boud, R Keogh and D Walker, Kogan Page, London

Clothier, P (1996) *The Complete Computer Trainer*, McGraw-Hill, New York

Cornish, C (1995) *Can You Hear Me at the Back?*, BiVocal Press, Exeter

Cunningham, P (1983) 'Helping students to extract meaning from experience' in *Helping Adults to Learn How to Learn, New Directions for Continuing Education*, No 19, (ed) R Smith, Jossey-Bass, San Francisco

Deshler, D (1990) 'Conceptual mapping: drawing charts of the mind' in *Fostering Critical Reflection in Adulthood*, ed J Mezirow, Jossey-Bass, San Francisco

Eisner, E (1991) 'Forms of understanding and the future of education', *Educational Researcher*, **22**, pp 5–11

Eizenberg, N (1988) 'Approaches to learning anatomy: developing a programme for medical students' in *Improving Learning*, ed P Ramsden, Kogan Page, London

Entwistle, N (1988) *Styles of Learning*, David Fulton, Edinburgh

Entwistle, N (1996), 'Recent research on student learning and the learning environment' in *The Management of Independent Learning*, eds J Tait and P Knight, SEDA/Kogan Page, London

Entwistle, A and Entwistle, N (1997) 'The experience of understanding in revising for degree examinations', *Learning and Instruction*, **2**, pp 1–22

Eraut, M (1994) *Developing Professional Knowledge and Competence*, Falmer, Brighton

Ertmer, P and Newby, T (1996) 'The expert learner: strategic, self-regulated and reflective', *Instructional Science*, **24**, pp 1–24

Forsyth, P (1992) *Running an Effective Training Session*, Gower, Aldershot

Fox, D (1983) 'Personal theories of teaching', *Studies in Higher Education*, **8** (2), pp 151–63

Gallway, T (1975) *The Inner Game of Tennis*, Jonathan Cape, London

Gardner, H (1983) *Frames of Mind – The Theory of Multiple Intelligences*, Basic Books, New York

Gayhe, A and Lillyman, S (1997), *Learning Journals and Critical Incidents*, Quay Books, Dinton

Gregorc, A (1973) 'Developing plans for professional growth', *NASSP Bulletin*, Dec 1973

Grumet, M (1987) 'The politics of personal knowledge', *Curriculum Inquiry*, **17**, (13), pp 319–35

Habermas, J (1971) *Knowledge and Human Interests*, Heinemann, London

Harri-Augstein, S and Thomas, L (1991) *Learning Conversations*, Routledge, London

Harrison, R (1991) Training and Development, *Institute of Personnel Management*, London

Hartley, J (1998) *Learning and Studying*, Routledge, London

Harvey, L and Knight, P (1996) *Transforming Higher Education*, SRHE/OUP, Buckingham

HEA, HEBS, HPW, HPANI (1995) *A Handbook on the Development of Foundation Courses in Health Promotion*, Health Promotion Wales, Cardiff

HECIW (Higher Education Credit Initiative, Wales) (1996, 2nd edn, 1999), *Welsh Higher Education Credit Framework Handbook,* Wales Access Unit, Cardiff

HECIW (1999), *Welsh Higher Education Credit Framework Handbook*, Higher Education Development, Wales, Cardiff

Honey, P and Mumford, A (1986) *Using Our Learning Styles*, Honey Publications, London

Jaques, D (1991) *Learning in Groups*, Kogan Page, London

Jessup, G (1991) *Outcomes, NVQs and the Emerging Model of Education and Training*, Falmer Press, London

Kelly, G (1955) *The Psychology of Personal Construct Theory, Vols 1 and 2*, Norton, New York

Kember, D (1996) 'The intention to memorise and understand: another approach to learning', *Higher Education*, **31**, pp 341–54

Kiely, M (1988) *A Study of the Impact of Health Education Certificate Courses*, PhD, Keele University

King, P and Kitchener, K (1994) *Developing Reflective Judgement*, Jossey-Bass, San Francisco

Kirby, A (1992) *Games for Trainers*, Gower, Aldershot

Kolb, D (1984) *Experiential Learning as the Science of Learning and Development*, Prentice Hall, Englewood Cliffs, New Jersey

Lawlor, M and Handley, P (1996) *The Creative Trainer*, McGraw-Hill, Maidenhead

Macaulay, C and Cree, V (1999) 'Transfer of learning: concept and process', *Social Work Education*, **18** (2), pp 183–93

McKay, J and Kember, D (1997) 'Spoon feeding leads to regurgitation: a better diet can result in more digestible learning outcomes', *Higher Education Research and Development*, **16** (1), pp 55–67

McLean, M and Blackwell, R (1997) 'Opportunity knocks? Professionalism and excellence in university teaching', *Teachers and Teaching: theory and practice*, **3** (1), pp 85–99

Martin, S and Darnley, L (1996) *The Teaching Voice*, Whurr Publishers, London

Marton, F, Hounsell, D and Entwistle, N (1997) *The Experience of Learning*, 2nd edn, Scottish Academic Press, Edinburgh

Marton, F and Ramsden, P (1988) 'What does it take to improve learning?' in *Improving Learning: New perspectives*, ed P Ramsden, Kogan Page, London

Marton, F and Saljo, R (1997) 'Approaches to learning' in *The Experience of Learning*, eds F Marton, D Hounsell and N Entwistle, Academic Press, Edinburgh

Moon, J (1976) 'Some thoughts on study skills', *Reading* **10**, pp 24–34

Moon, J (1996) 'What can you do in a day?' Advice on developing short training courses on promotiong health, *Journal of the Institute of Health Promotion*, **34** (1), pp 20–23

Moon, J (1998) *Towards Purpose, Clarity and Effectiveness in Training, Teaching and Learning* paper towards the award of PhD, Oct 1998, University of Glamorgan

Moon, J (1999) *Reflection in Learning and Professional Development*, Kogan Page, London

Moon, J (1999a) *Learning Journals, a handbook for academics, students and professional development*, London, Kogan Page

Moon, J and England, P (1994) 'The development of a highly structured workshop in health promotion', *Journal of the Inst of Health Promotion*, **32** (2), pp 41–44

Morgan, N, Saxon, S (1991) *Teaching Questioning and Learning*, Routledge, London

NCIHE, (1997), *Report of the National Committee of Inquiry into Higher Education* (the 'Dearing Report'), NCIHE, London

Oates, L, and Watson, L (1996) 'Providing the instructional infrastructure to support flexible learning' in *Enabling Student Learning: systems and strategies,* eds G Wisker and S Brown, SEDA/Kogan Page, London

Odum, E (1968*) Ecology*, Holt, Rhinehart and Winston, New York

Parlett, M and King, J (1971) *Concentrated Study*, SRHE, London

Pask, G (1976) 'Styles and strategies of learning', B J of *Ed Psych*, **46**, pp 4–11

Perry, W (1970) *Forms of Intellectual and Academic Development in College Years,* Holt, Rhinehart and Winston, New York

Piaget, J (1971) *Biology and Knowledge*, Edinburgh University Press, Edinburgh

Pinar, W (1975) 'Currere: towards recapitulation' in *Curriculum Theorizing,* ed W Pinar, McCutcham Publishing Corp, Berkley, CA

Pithers, R (1998) *Improving learning through effective training,* Social Science Press, Katoomba, Australia

Polyani, M (1966) *The Tacit Dimension,* Doubleday, New York

Pont, T (1991) *Developing Effective Training Skills*, McGraw-Hill Training Series, Maidenhead, Berks

Prosser, M, Trigwell, K and Taylor, P (1994) 'A phenomenographic study of academics' conceptions of science teaching and learning', *Learning and Instruction*, **4**, pp 217–31

Reid, M, Barrington, H and Kenney, J (1992) *Training Interventions*, Institute of Personnel Management, London

Rawlins, M (1999) Personal communication

Robson, M (1993) *Problem-Solving in Groups*, Gower, Aldershot

Rogers, C (1969) *Freedom to Learn*, Charles E Merrill, Columbus, Ohio

Rose, C (1985) *Accelerated Learning,* Topaz Publishing Ltd, Great Missenden, Bucks

Russell, T (1994) *Effective Feedback Skill*, Kogan Page, London

Schein, E (1988) *Process Consultation Vol 1*, Addison-Wesley, Reading, MA

Schön, D (1983) *The Reflective Practitioner,* Jossey-Bass, San Francisco

Schön, D (1987) Educating the Reflective Practitioner, Jossey-Bass, San Francisco

Schuck, G (1996) 'Intelligent technology, intelligent workers' in *How Organizations Learn,* ed K Starkey, Thomson Business Press, London

Schuell, T (1986) 'Cognitive conceptions of learning', *Rev Ed Res* (56), pp 411–36

Sheal, P (1989) *How to Develop and Present Staff Training Courses*, Kogan Page, London

Sotto, E (1994) *When Teaching Becomes Learning*, Cassell, London

Steinaker, N and Bell, R (1979) *The Experiential Taxonomy: a new approach to teaching and learning,* Academic Press, New York

Taylor, I (1997) *Developing Learning in Professional Education*, SRHE/OUP, Buckingham

Thomas, B (1992) *Total Quality Training*, McGraw-Hill, London

Tobin, K (1987) 'The role of wait time in higher cognitive learning', *Review of Educational Research,* **57**, pp 69–75

Trigwell M, Prosser, K (1999) *Understanding Learning and Teaching,* SRHE/OUP, Buckingham

Usher, R (1985) 'Beyond the anecdotal: adult learning and the use of experience', *Studies in the Education of Adults,* **17** (1), pp 59–74

Van Manen, M (1977) 'Linking ways of knowing with ways of being', *Curriculum Inquiry,* **6**, pp 205–08

Van Manen, M (1991) *The Tact of Teaching,* The State of New York Press, New York

Van Ments, M (1990) *Active Talk,* Kogan Page, London

Van Rossum, E and Schenk S (1984) 'The relationship between learning conception, study strategy and learning outcome', *British Journal of Educational Psychology,* **54**, 73–83

Waldman, J, Glover, N and King, E (1999) 'Readiness to Learn', *Social Work Education,* **18** (2), pp 219–28

Wetherell, J, and Mullins, G (1996) 'The use of student journals in problem-based learning', *Medical Education,* 30, pp 105–11

Winitzky, N and Kauchak, D (1997) 'Constructivism in teacher education: applying cognitive theory to teacher learning' in *Constructivist Teacher Training,* ed V Richardson, Falmer Press, London

Willis, M (1993) *Managing the Training Process,* McGraw-Hill, Maidenhead

Zuber-Skerritt, O (1992) *Professional Development in Higher Education: a theoretical framework for action research,* Kogan Page, London

Index